The Blue Collar Thoroughbred

The Blue Collar Thoroughbred

An Inside Account of the Real World of Racing

Gene McCormick

McFarland & Company, Inc., Publishers
Jefferson, North Carolina, and London

The author has also written two chess books: *The U.S. Chess Championship, 1845–1985* (McFarland, 1986), by Gene H. McCormick and Andy Soltis (second edition, *1845–1996*, by Andy Soltis and Gene H. McCormick; McFarland, 1997), and *Bird's Defense to the Ruy Lopez* (McFarland, 1981).

Photographs by Kathy Curtice. Chapter 7 originally appeared in a different form as "Retraining the Veteran Racehorse," *Illinois Racing News* (Sept. 2006): 22–23.

LIBRARY OF CONGRESS CATALOGUING-IN-PUBLICATION DATA

McCormick, Gene H., 1940–
The blue collar thoroughbred : an inside account of the real world of racing / Gene McCormick.
p. cm.
Includes index.

ISBN-13: 978-0-7864-3049-9
(softcover : 50# alkaline paper) ∞

1. Horse racing. 2. Thoroughbred horse. I. Title.
SF334.M35 2007
798.4—dc22 2007007487

British Library cataloguing data are available

On the cover: "Call Me Loverboy," 11" × 14" watercolor by Judith Berkshire Jones

Manufactured in the United States of America

McFarland & Company, Inc., Publishers
Box 611, Jefferson, North Carolina 28640
www.mcfarlandpub.com

Acknowledgments

As this is a work of non-fiction, it was essential that the subjects in *The Blue Collar Thoroughbred* first lived the roles and then proved gracious enough to publicly share chapters of their lives.

Call Me Loverboy, the title subject, communicated his story in a number of ways but primarily on the track, his reward for cooperation being carrots, mints, rubs and admiration. Other equine heroes such as Dr. Robbie, Fusto, Chindi, Awholelotofmalarky, Are You Dancing and Captain Fluffy let their caretakers have the final words.

Jockeys Earlie Fires, Newil Wall, Dudley Vandenborre and Randy Meier opened up the mysteries of race riding as seldom detailed previously through their talented eyes, hands and reins that have cumulatively accounted for more than 10,000 wins.

Man-about-the-track Dan Arrigo, who always treated Call Me Loverboy with respect, was the inspiration for these chronicles. His track-wise knowledge could fill a set of equine *Encyclopaedia Britannicas*, while his roundtable owner and trainer friends Sharyn Cole, Ron and Bev Goodridge, George and Mary Kazarian, Pam Little, Dan and Patty Miller, Jan Ely, Steve Hobby, Paul Lewellyn and Robert Weiner helped demystify the sport and filled in the occasional blank.

Ralph Martinez, a young trainer in a hurry, always took ample time to thoroughly discuss relevant activities in a sport where cloak-and-dagger secrecies are as much the norm as honesty and candor.

Joan Colby, in her capacity as editor of the *Illinois Racing News,* shared her extensive background information regarding Midwest horse racing, while Tower Farm's Wally and Janet Hartwig offered an enlightening glimpse into dreams coming true. Morgan McDonnell's own Derby dreams may or may not come to fruition, and sometimes when you do everything as it should be done it just doesn't really matter.

Thanks to handicapping cronies Jim Settembre and Clarence "Buddy" Qualls, whose racetrack tips always provided comic if not financial relief. More substantive information was always at hand daily, weekly and hopefully in perpetuity through *The Blood-Horse,* the *Thoroughbred Times,* the *Illinois Racing News* and the *Daily Racing Form.*

The chapter on Chindi, "How You Gonna Keep 'Em Down on the Farm...?" originally appeared in the *Illinois Racing News* in slightly different format.

The Blue Collar Thoroughbred is dedicated to Jake and Roxanne, beloved and loving family members who couldn't be around for the final chapter. My wife Marie and our sweetheart Sarah had to take up the slack, as did Toby with his well-intended but biting criticisms, and they did so admirably. But none of this would have been possible without the continuing support of my partner, Kathy, who also took the photographs appearing throughout the book.

Table of Contents

Table of Contents

Introduction

The Blue Collar Thoroughbred is a nonfiction insider biography of today's sport of Thoroughbred racing, breeding and riding from a broad stroke, day-to-day, behind the scenes vantage point.

The chronicle is apportioned into three unequal but not unrelated sections: racing, breeding, and riding, or jockeying. The names, places and activities change in each segment, but just as a roadmap shows different streets leading to a common destination, each segment ultimately brings the reader closer to the truth and relevance of horseracing.

Thoroughbred racing has always been a magnificent and mercurial sport but should no longer be considered, contrary to what has become chiseled in archival racing lore, the "Sport of Kings." It is democratic, more bourgeois than royal, actively engaged in and enjoyed by multitudes from all levels of the social and business strata of life, a mix in which a furniture store owner or used car dealer or beer distributor can pit his horse against that of a queen or a sheik and sit side by side in an owner's box. It is the best horse that will win, not the wealthiest owner.

Of course it is those with the big bank accounts at the very tip of the sport who can afford the highest stud fees when breeding, can buy the top-priced mega-million yearlings at auction, and can ship their horses globally from stakes race to stakes race. This book documents how the other ninety-five percent of Thoroughbred racing live, thrive and care about horses that always seem to run on the undercard Monday through Friday, but almost never on Saturday when the more bountiful stakes are run.

This is how racing happens.

—Gene McCormick
March 2007

Prologue

Dice clattered across the slippery cardboard surface, stopping at the edge of the board. The numbers totaled eight the hard way, two fours. The shooter shrugged. No matter. The Trivial Pursuit game piece was advanced eight squares, stopping on a sports question. It was a mock serious game being played for bragging rights, guys against girls, and the ladies could win with a correct answer. It was a baseball question and the only answer they knew, Babe Ruth, was incorrect. The guys grabbed at the dice, rolling vigorously and with raucous authority, but their reprieve proved temporary. Forced to answer a science question, they found that "Albert Einstein" ("The Babe Ruth of science!") was not a universal answer. Taking their turn, shaking the dice with tight-lipped determination, the girls were required to answer another sports question, this one about horseracing. Their answer, again the only one they knew, was Secretariat. It was the correct response.

Prologue

Ruth and Secretariat are icons of their sports, subconscious answers-in-waiting on the tips of the tongues of games players and sports fans alike. Their feats and legends have bolted from yesterday's headlines to become immortalized in board games, Halls of Fame, books, movies and television documentaries, all serving to indelibly etch awareness into even the most casual of sports fans worldwide. The two heroes were total opposites: Ruth was an overweight, moon-faced orphan scamp who had hit more home runs by the time he retired than any player in history. Secretariat was far better bred and much more handsome than the Babe, behaved himself on and off the track with aplomb and set Triple Crown track records that still stand. The Babe and Big Red may have come from different worlds and competed in different sports but their effect on the sporting and general public was singular.

It is the team concept, however, that drives people to the ballpark. Fans go to the stadiums to see a team compete, not an individual player. The superstars of the sport will always offer a certain allure en route to becoming trivia question answers but it is the entire team that wins pennants and World Series. While only a handful of players have achieved anything close to Ruthian status, most baseball players are capable of hitting an occasional home run just as most Thoroughbreds can win at least a race or two, if not the Kentucky Derby, Preakness or Belmont Stakes. As it is the team that defines baseball, it is the team, or mass, of common horses that sustains racing; that comprises the platform for daily gambling action, which in turn generates purse money for successful Thoroughbreds, which in turn encourages promulgation of the breed, thereby renewing the cycle that every decade or two produces a truly memorable horse. Casual horse fans and devotees alike turn out in big numbers to see the stars of the sport compete against one another in Saturday stakes action but it is the hard-core gamblers, the Betting People, who keep the sport fiscally viable by gambling Sunday through Friday at a racetrack or at off-track betting shops.

This book chronicles everyday blue-collar lunch-pail Thoroughbreds and those who depend on them to grind out a livelihood. It is an inside story of the middle-and-lower-echelon runners that compete when the television cameras are turned off, and it is a story of trainers who drive well-traveled, rusted pickup trucks with cracked windshields and of jockeys whose Sunday best is blue denim and of owners who hope the check for their next feed bill clears. To these horses and caretakers the pursuit of a win, of sustaining a career in their chosen way of life with an occasional highlight, is anything but trivial.

These unsung horses run just as hard as the vaunted marquee Thoroughbreds competing for million-dollar purses. The difference is that it takes the meat-and-potatoes guys a little longer to get to the finish line; to the winner's circle.

Most of the activity described in the pages that follow took place between 2001 and 2006, but it could have been almost any time. It could not have been any place, however. It could only have been on the race track.

I

At the Track

Call Me Loverboy with regular jockey Eusabio "Eddie" Razo, Jr., wearing the silks of J & J Stable.

I. At the Track

First horse to the finish line wins, about as simple as a sporting objective can be. But few things are ever quite so simple as they appear, and winning a horse race is no exception. Unlike most major team sports such as baseball, football, basketball and soccer in which one team only has to beat one opponent to win the contest (which is accomplished with the help of teammates), or one-on-one individual contests such as boxing, tennis, bowling, and—for all most of us know—tiddlywinks, a racehorse must outrun numerous opponents, usually eight to twelve and frequently more, occasionally less, while carrying approximately 120 pounds of passenger and equipment.

Unlike its sporting cousin auto racing, a tired or out-of-tune Thoroughbred cannot simply get an oil change and a new carburetor installed. Broken or damaged parts cannot be pulled from a shelf and installed as needed. Infinitely more care and training are required to get a racehorse to make a few left turns around a racing oval faster than other 1,000-pound animals running flat-out shoulder to shoulder with him at upwards of forty miles an hour.

Pssst... Anybody Wanna Buy a Horse?

In the fall of 2005 a young, well-bred and well-raced mare recently retired from her duties as a racehorse was sold for a world record $9,000,000 at the premier auction in the country, Keeneland, in Lexington, Kentucky. The jaw-dropping sale price was apparently benefited by a bidding war between an oil country sheikh and an international breeding conglomerate. The average price for the 2,819 Thoroughbreds sold at the Keeneland sale of breeding stock was $102,733.

A few weeks later Chicago horseman Dan Arrigo was preparing to hold his annual paddock sale of horses of racing age at Hawthorne Race Course near Chicago's inner city. The average sale price realized at Arrigo's paddock sale would not pay the sales tax on a Keeneland sales horse, but two of the most successful trainers in the world would be in the Hawthorne paddock bidding, looking for winning stock.

I. At the Track

Distant equine thunder was rolling closer now, and a few, say half, of the dozen or so onlookers—the hard core Betting People—looked up at the race in progress on the in-house television system, dropped their cigarettes, mashing them into the dull linoleum flooring while snapping their fingers in an out-of-sync cadence with the horse's lengthening stride. C'*mon* with that seven horse, whip his ass, jock, get *into* him, you got it, you *got* it, you GOT it....

Horse and rider were oblivious to any noises from the bettors, most of whom were ensconced behind the noise-muffling glass-enclosed stands watching the race through the benefit and comfort of electronics. It was early April on the south side of Chicago and it was a typically cold, blustery mid-week spring day at Hawthorne Race Course. No more than twenty chilled people were outside, strung out along the rail, shoulders hunched up to their ears, watching with cursory interest as the stretch finale of the $6,000 claiming race played out.

But the seven horse was totally attuned to the moment and the task at hand, and the rider as well. Slow to break from the gate, the blood bay was now driving through the stretch, powering like an out-of-control downhill roller coaster, the finish line a few gasps away. Horse after horse was being left behind. The equine comet's black mane and tail were horizontal, whipping about from the aerodynamic rush. His ears were pinned flat to his head and his legs hammered at the track with the force and determination of sledgehammers pounding railroad spikes, mutilating—branding—the surface with indelible hoof prints, spewing surface loam about the track. The Thoroughbred's breath was both audible and visible—*hunhh, hunhh, hunhh*—his nostrils flared as round as saucers and the muscles and blood vessels in his head were throbbing, pulsating to a near-bursting point under the blinkered hood worn to keep his attention to the job at hand. Such artifice was unnecessary; the horse was so tightly focused he couldn't begin to feel pain from the sting of the crouching jockey's whip first hitting one flank and then the other, impossibly asking for more with each lash. The burning in his lungs and legs was ignored, as was the kicked-up dirt from the track that was stinging his eyes like an assault of needle pricks. It didn't matter to the horse that he may have a new owner at the end of the race, that unfamiliar hands may be caring for him, or that he could be sleeping in a strange stall. Churning ever forward, the big horse knew his job and nothing was going to stop him from getting to the wire first. Nothing.

After the race, with the lathered horse in the winner's circle impatiently posing for the track photographer, lifting first one aching leg and then another, a rival trainer shrugged off the race. "I knew the seven could win it if he finishes the race, but he's got a knee looks like a freakin' roadmap and ankles bigger than my girlfriend's thighs. No way I drop a claim."

Deep within the bowels of the racetrack in a subterranean paddock lacking both natural light and air flow, hardened racetrack lifer Dan Arrigo was conducting his annual pickle auction. In track parlance a "pickle" is a Thoroughbred who is generally unwanted and untalented, for any number of reasons: injury, age, lack of speed, attitude or general wear and tear. Hawthorne Race Course, host site for Arrigo's paddock auction of horses of racing age, is a midlevel venue with just enough stature that horses deemed no longer suitable for competition at Hawthorne may still have dollar value at tracks a bit further down in the pecking order, such as Fairmount, Thistledown, Great Lakes Downs or Mountaineer, among others.

It is not unusual for tracks or horse-trading entrepreneurs to conduct or encourage such an auction at the end of a meet. Paddock sales give stables a chance to either unload unwanted stock or to bulk up their stables with horses possessing at least a modicum of upside. Pedigrees are of minimal significance in this type of a sale as most of the stock consists of aged geldings with no breeding value or stallions with racing records so dismal as to preclude any desire on the part of prospective breeders to repeat the bloodlines. The few fillies or mares on offer rarely have lineage that would encourage breeders to take a chance with proliferation. At a paddock sale the bidder is gambling on what the horse may do on the track in the future, not his bloodlines nor what he has already accomplished. As one of the bid spotters noted, "You are bidding on the horse, not its winnings." Wearing an olive drab camouflage outfit confidently set off by a pancake-sized rodeo prize belt buckle that made an in-your-face statement, the spotter was cracking an auction joke but the wisdom of a life on the track was in his wisecrack. An aware buyer will be studying a horse's past performance lines in the *Daily Racing Form* and checking out the tell-tale lumps and bumps on the horse's legs rather than scoping out a four-generation pedigree.

The man responsible for assembling the auction, cajoling entries from reluctant owners or trainers, producing the 18-page photocopied catalog, tacking up eye-catching yellow flyers citing rules and regulations and for pre-registering and checking the credit of the seventy-five or so potential bidders is a racetrack habitué as familiar to Chicago backstretch workers as the Sears Tower is to the Loop's skyline.

Dan Arrigo has been making his living by hanging around race tracks since grade school, more than half a century ago. Now in his mid-sixties, he still has the smooth hands of a man used to making his living with his head, not by hard labor. If Arrigo were to put together a resume, page one would start with his having swept out the grandstand as an eight-year-old while hawking horse shoes worn by such yesteryear fan favorites as Native Dancer ("The Dancer would have to have been an equine centipede to have worn as many shoes as I sold"). His career progressed in steady fashion for a racetracker, advancing to gofer, hot walker and groom, all the while getting hands-on, entry-level horse-learning from employers such as

***Opposite*: Dan Arrigo personifies the racetrack "lifer." He began working at the track as a juvenile, studying the *Daily Racing Form* while other kids his age had paper routes and concerned themselves with homework and hooky. Arrigo has been a gofer, hotwalker, groom, assistant trainer, trainer, auctioneer, and bloodstock agent, having bought and sold thousands of horses privately or through auctions.**

1. Psst... Anybody Wanna Buy a Horse?

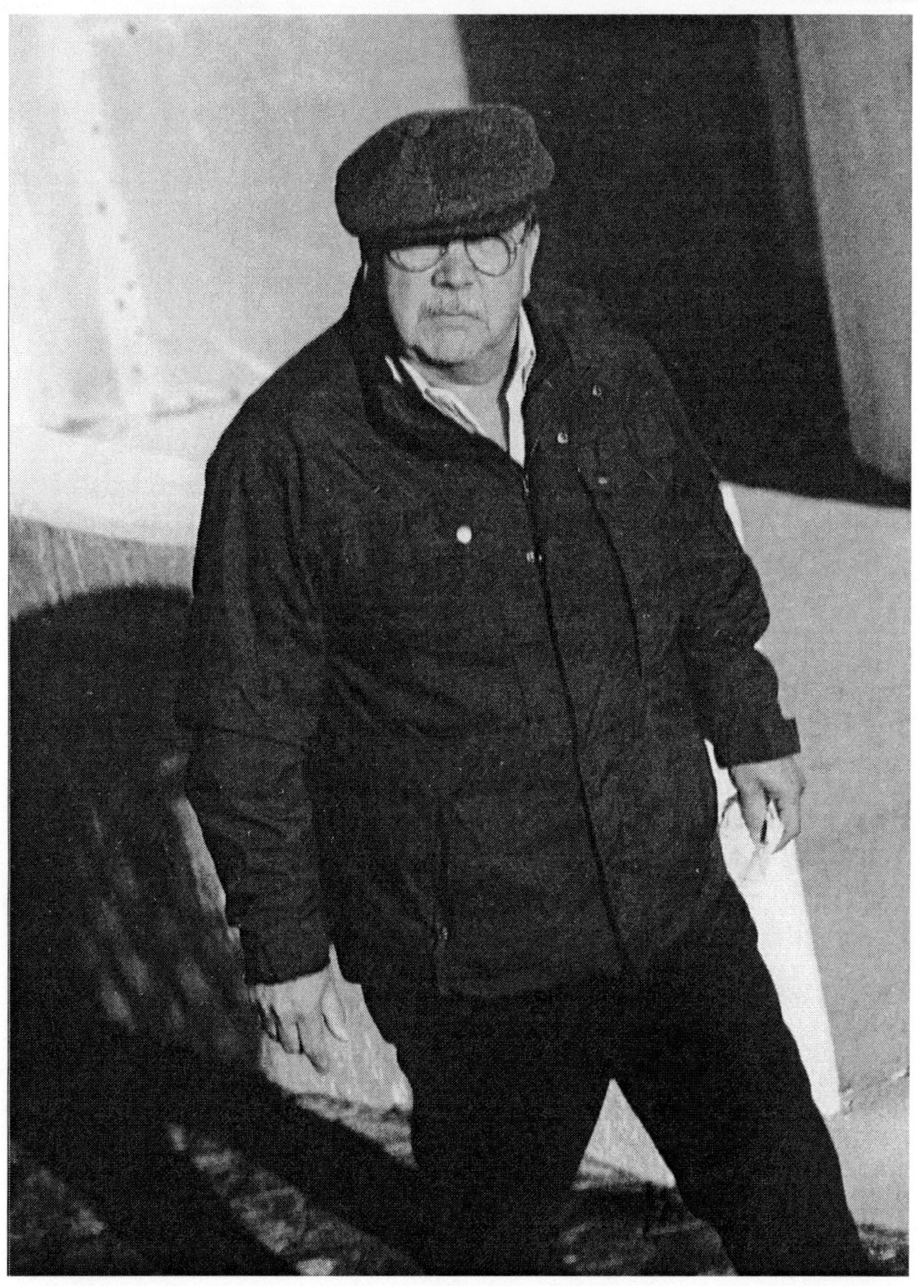

Hall of Fame trainer Marion Van Berg (father of Hall of Fame trainer Jack Van Berg) and other Midwest training legends. "Working for Van Berg was easy," said Arrigo, "because you only worked half days: from sunup to sundown." Van Berg was reportedly such a stickler for details that after a groom mucked out a stall and spread new bedding around, "Mr. Van" would take a yardstick into the stall and measure the depth of the straw from corner to corner to make certain it was spread evenly.

With a thorough grounding in track and training basics, Arrigo eventually switched to the jockey's side of horseracing, becoming a jockey's agent, hustling mounts for such 1950s and '60s A-list names as Hank Moreno, Ray York, Milo Valenzuela (best known for having replaced Eddie Arcaro as the regular rider of five-time Horse of the Year Kelso), and others whose exploits have now become just memories etched on yellowing winner's circle pictures. For years Arrigo led the nomadic life of a jockey agent, living out of a suitcase as he traveled the Illinois, Florida, California and Louisiana racing circuits, cadging rides for his clients and establishing a reputation among owners and trainers for being a man of his word and for honoring commitments, which is not considered a job requirement for the typical agent.

By the mid–1980s Arrigo had mentally and physically had enough of the grinding road life, tensions and the constant barn-to-barn hustling necessary to get trainers to commit a mount to his jock. "Actually I liked everything about being a jock's agent, but after years of doing it, it just got cumulatively tiresome and too much like work than fun, so it was time to think of something different." After a brief fling at running a tack shop, he decided to meld his diverse experiences into what was at the time a unique form of horse trading. Arrigo became a bloodstock agent ("horse trader") primarily buying and selling racing-age breeding stock claimed at tracks throughout the country.

Working out of a basement office in his comfortable north side suburban Chicago split-level, Arrigo electronically tracks as many as 700 horses on a daily basis, virtually all of which are fillies or mares. His bulging file cabinets contain records of a minimum of 150 transactions a year, and bookcases lining the wood-paneled walls hold a decade's worth of auction sales records, several years of the *Daily Racing Form,* and *American Produce Records.* Essential equipment includes a computer loaded with Windows 98 software outfitted with a customized tracking system, a fax machine, a printer, and several telephones. Seven days a week Arrigo scans through his system, checking the *Form*, locating fillies and mares running in claiming races and then crosschecking their pedigrees and dam-side produce record in the *American Produce Records.* "I only track claiming races," says Arrigo, "because I can't buy, or claim, a horse from an allowance or stakes race. And I only look at fillies and mares. Realistically, a promising stallion wouldn't be running in a claiming race." A horse is eliminated from consideration if it has been consistently running at the same claiming price, or if the price has gone up. "If the horse stays at the same price level," he says, "it means that I looked at her before, as have my competitors, and didn't claim her. So, if we weren't interested at the earlier price we're not going to be interested at a higher price. Of course, there are exceptions. I passed on a mare running in mid-level claiming races in Florida, and then again in Canada, that turned out to be a full sister to Kickin' Kris, who won the Grade 1 Secretariat last year and the Grade 1 Arlington Million this year."

Because Arrigo claims horses with the intention of breeding or reselling rather than racing, he can gamble a long-distance, sight-unseen claim on a filly or mare. The claiming game is largely a business of secrets, subterfuge and deception. Are the front wraps on a Thoroughbred's legs there because of necessity, for prevention, or for misdirection? Are the joints of an aged horse going to hold together for a few more races? Has the horse been stopping in his races because of a wind or bleeding problem, or is he just track-sore? Trainers with gambling instincts and ice water for blood who think they know the answers to such secrets are the most successful claiming trainers. Arrigo's biggest concern is that the horse he just claimed successfully make it around the track one final time before being led off to the breeding shed or auction house.

Should Arrigo decide to claim an out-of-state horse he is usually able to find a willing associate at that particular track who is eligible to enter claims, and who can advise on any glaring physical deficiencies the horse may have. Money for the claim has to be sent, typically by wire transfer, to the track prior to the claim's being submitted. If Arrigo successfully claims the horse, all that remains to be done is to arrange shipping to one of the several farms he contracts with to function as a holding area until he can either resell the horse or get it to auction. On rare occasions he will train and race the horse.

As a supplement to his nationwide computer tracking system, Arrigo actively works the Chicago tracks, personally arranging private, non-claiming, above-board but under-the-radar buy-sell transactions that occasionally involve up to several dozen horses at a time.

In addition to negotiating buy and sell deals for himself and various clients, for more than ten years Arrigo has been conducting periodic horses-of-racing-age auctions, the so-called pickle sales, at Hawthorne and other tracks. The auction Arrigo was currently running had 35 horses entered, an average number for such a sale. Some of the Thoroughbreds would be going to other trainers at other tracks; some would wind up as riding horses, or hunters if they were sound enough. None, if Arrigo could help it, would go to the killers, the slaughterhouse agents who attend bottom-of-the-barrel auctions hoping to buy a horse cheap enough to resell to slaughterhouses at a profit. Arrigo sets the minimum bid high enough to discourage killer bids.

As busy as Arrigo was with last-minute registrations and renewed acquaintances, putting on a paddock sale is far from being a one-man show. Seven assistants hired just for the day were purposefully going about their pre-auction preparations which included everything from slapping a self-sticking identification number on a horse's rear flank—thereby called the "hip number"—to strategically placing industrial-sized trash baskets and planters to form an oblong area in the paddock, a space approximately 25' x 40', which would function as the showcase walking ring for the horses to be auctioned. A four-man auctioneering staff was in place to handle auction-in-progress activities such as bid spotting (a bid spotter identifies the current bidder for the auctioneer) and untangling any buyer confusions. There were no seats for the bidders, who were casually milling about behind temporary white plastic chain barriers, occasionally stomping their feet and slapping their hands together to keep warm. The auction would begin at 10:30 A.M. and would be over in two hours, ending in time for Arrigo to make a bank deposit before the end of the business day.

Coming as it does between Christmas and New Year's, there was an aura of camaraderie and good cheer among the 75 or so in attendance, many of whom knew one another, but there was also a look of quiet anticipation among those who figured to be bidding. It was a male-dominated group, nearly all of whom were casually dressed in quilted down jackets, blue jeans, work boots and baseball caps. Fewer than a third could be considered potential bidders. The stock they would be attempting to acquire—castoffs from other stables—represented short- and mid-term future revenue and would directly affect the livelihood of the new owners and trainers. With claiming horses there is usually no long-term anticipation.

The first several horses through the ring sold for minimum bids, just high enough to keep the killers at bay. The low bids were evidence that the past performance lines on those horses didn't forecast a bright racing future; indeed, the young ladies who successfully bid on the first several horses intended to use them as riding horses. As Thoroughbreds with better racing resumes entered the ring it didn't take long for the bidding action to heat up.

Unobtrusively leaning against concrete pillars at opposite ends of the walking ring from one another, waiting for horses that might

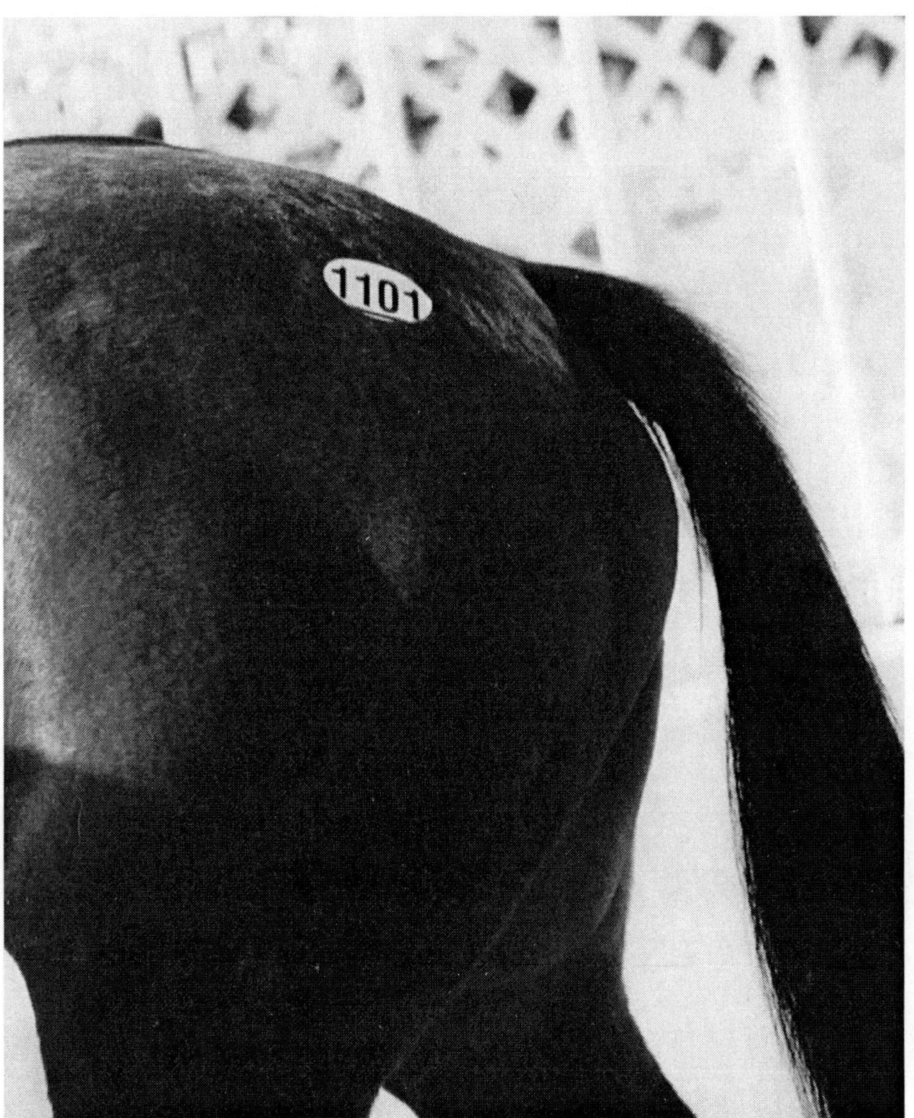

For identification purposes, a number is attached to the hip of a horse being auctioned. The auctioneer will refer to a horse by its hip number, not its name (in fact, most weanlings and yearlings being auctioned do not have a name at the time of the auction).

fit into their extensive racing stables to go into the ring, were two of the winningest trainers in the country.

Dale Baird has in fact won more races in the *world* than any trainer in history. Stabled at Mountaineer Park, a relatively new racino (race track and casino) located in Chester, West Virginia, that was formerly known as Waterford Park in a previous incarnation, for the last 33 of his 40-plus years as a trainer, the sixty-nine-year-old Baird has won 15 national leading trainer titles based on number of wins; he has been the leading owner by races won 17 times; was the first trainer to win 300 races in a year; and he has saddled an average of four winners a week during his career. Through 2003 Baird had won a total of 8,884 races and the watershed 9,000-win mark was to be just a matter of time. His unprecedented feats have earned him recognition in the *Guinness Book of World Records*, and in 2001 he was inducted into the Horsemen's Benevolent and Protective Association's Hall of Fame. Despite these accomplishments Baird is not a familiar name to the average race-goer because nearly all his feats have been performed in racing's outback, at lesser tracks that seldom feature major stakes races, and he has racked up his totals with less-than-prime-time horses.

At this stage of his career Baird had not driven eight nonstop hours from West Virginia looking for Eclipse winners, nor had he made the trek looking to buy no-potential pickles. Despite his arguably world-class accomplishments Baird was still hungry enough to have driven across three states to a dreary mid-winter paddock sale in an attempt to pick up a few more usable horses at the right price. He came to replenish his hard-knocking stock with some Thoroughbreds that could win races on the purse-rich but talent-challenged Mountaineer circuit, and Baird is known to have an eye for evaluating a horse. Having been around race horses his entire life, the trainer could spot a horse's flaws in a nanosecond, and he knew that there were no perfect specimens in Arrigo's sale. What Baird was looking for were horses that had attractive racing "conditions" left. (A condition reflects the level of eligibility a horse has.

For example, a horse that has never won a race is eligible to enter maiden races. A horse that has never won more than one race can be entered in a race for "non-winners of a race other than maiden, or non-winners of two races lifetime," and so on. The more conditions a horse is eligible for, the better chances of picking up a few quick purses. When a horse has run through its conditions it must compete in open allowance, claiming or stakes races, which represent a more difficult level of opposition for most horses). Because a portion of the profits from legalized gambling at the casino were used to augment racing prize money, purses at Mountaineer had grown out of proportion with the quality of the horses competing. Baird was well aware that, given a racing-sound horse with at least a few conditions left, he could win some quick, purse-fat races back in West Virginia.

Fifty feet away from Baird, partially sheltered by a concrete pillar and a waist-high industrial wastebasket, wearing a sweatshirt, faded blue jeans and a baseball cap pulled low over his eyes, a horseman more than forty years Baird's junior would also be bidding, and he was also a trainer with a plan.

Still in his mid-twenties, Ralph Martinez was far from inclined to boast he had done it all. Quick to smile and just as modest and unassuming as Baird, Martinez would never begin to acknowledge that he had accomplished anything other than the residual end result of hard work and diligence, even though his early results indicate that he is on a fast track to put up some Baird-like numbers. Since he took over as private trainer for Louis O'Brien's Shamrock Stable in 2000, Martinez has had success. "My father, Raul, had been Mr. O'Brien's trainer but when my younger sister was killed in an accident in 2000 it had a lingering effect on my father, and I started to manage the stable for Mr. O'Brien. My father gave me the blueprint, and Mr. O'Brien gives me the horses."

It was evident that the younger Martinez had learned his lessons well, not least by the fact that his 2003 win totals had put him in the national top ten. In the fall of the year Martinez had set the

Hoosier Park record for number of wins in a single season (65, easily surpassing the former record of 42), and he had previously been the leading trainer at Fairmount Park in downstate Illinois. His Hoosier Park record included a run of at least one win during 15 consecutive racing nights, and he scored three wins on one race card on four separate occasions. Martinez downplayed his record-setting skein: "It's cool," he said. "It's good to have the horses run so good. But we don't set goals, or have objectives other than to try to make Mr. O'Brien the leading owner at every track we run."

Not yet thirty years old, Ralph Martinez has become a familiar face among the top ten trainers ranked by the number of races won annually. Primarily competing at smaller tracks throughout the Midwest, Martinez deploys his stock as strategically as a chess master plots his moves.

Martinez works with claiming stock for the most part, and he quickly and of necessity has learned how to evaluate and correctly place his horses where they had the best chance to win. He approached Arrigo's horse auction much as a football coach might diagram a play on a chalkboard. Long before the auctioneer's hammer fell on the first hip number Martinez knew which horses he was going to bid on, how much he was willing to pay, and, displaying uncanny foresight, even where and when they would be entered in a race.

Hip number 994 (though there were only 35 horses in the sale, the hip numbers quirkily ranged from 890 to 1014) was a six-year-old club-footed gelding named Dr. Robbie. The flashy but shopworn chestnut had raced 68 times, finishing in the money half the time, and had earned $172,055, the most winnings of any horse entered in the sale. He had spent most of his career running in claiming races, peaking out at a $17,500 claiming price. Despite the handicap of a clubfoot, he was considered an honest horse that tried every time out. As a result, he had been claimed on ten separate occasions. In his two most recent races he had dropped to the lowest claiming rung at Hawthorne and could have been bought for $4,000 with no takers. Dr. Robbie had finished last in those races, beaten by 38½ and by 22¼ lengths, respectively. "Nothing really physically wrong with the horse," said trainer and consigner Jerry Gryczewski. "He's just a little sour. What he needs most of all is to be turned out for a few months R and R."

A $4,000 claiming horse with a deformed foot and a crappy attitude that had been beaten by 60 lengths the last two times out is not every trainer's idea of a meal ticket, but Martinez had vision and a plan, and when the hammer fell on #994 Martinez was high bidder on a soon-to-be-seven-year-old desperately in need of an attitude adjustment. The horse sold for $2,300, slightly more than half of his recent claiming value, but if Martinez' plan came to fruition Dr. Robbie would prove to be a tremendous bargain. "I plan to turn him out for a while," said the trainer. "Get him good and fresh, get his confidence level up, and then bring him back for a marathon series at Ellis Park later in the summer. The purse for the series final is $25,000, and last year the winner won by about thirty lengths because the only competition he had was from some maiden claimers. Dr. Robbie loves to run long, so he shouldn't have a problem with the marathon distance. If he gets any part of the purse he will more than have earned his selling price back after just a few months in the barn." Martinez had done his homework, plucking a potential big earner out of a discards sale and pointing him toward a race eight months in the future. Dr. Robbie had won at distances up to a mile and 9⁄16; his average winning distance was nearly a mile-and-a-half. As the saying goes, "When in the zoo, study your beasts," and Martinez had done some studying.

Martinez's second acquisition, a 1999 Majestie's Imp bay named Fusto, was a totally different proposition. Early in his career Fusto had shown some promise, selling for $20,000 as a two-year-old in an Illinois auction for horses of racing age. As a three-year-old he had won $74,460, three-and-a-half times his purchase price, but the horse had gone wrong when running on the lead in the 2002 Demetrisboy Stakes, a stakes race restricted to horses bred in Illinois. Off for nearly a year, Fusto came back and ran four times in 2003, all in six-furlong sprints at claiming prices from $18,000 down to $6,000. He was able to blast to the lead in each race only to fade badly in the stretch. The horse's earnings for the year totaled $50.00, about enough to pay his annual owner's license fee. Though he was once a financial asset, his connections now felt Fusto's usefulness as a racehorse was at an end, at least on the Chicago circuit where cheap races of less than six furlongs are seldom scheduled.

Once again thinking ahead, Martinez believed the horse was still sound enough to run short, and that he could maintain his speed for four or five furlongs, making him competitive at Fairmount Park, which scheduled a high percentage of short sprint races. When the auctioneer pounded down the gavel on #1009 after some brief but spirited bidding, Fusto belonged to Martinez' patron, Louis O'Brien, for $5,500. This time Martinez had a different strategy mapped out.

No sooner had the new ownership papers been signed than Fusto was on a van headed to Turfway Park in Florence, Kentucky, a one-mile circumference track with a short 970-yard stretch. Four days after being sold at auction Fusto carried O'Brien's Shamrock Stable silks in a five-furlong claiming race at Turfway. The horse broke well and led from the start, faltering within the sixteenth pole to lose a photo finish. The purse money for second place didn't cover his sales price, but it made a good dent. Martinez had the Turfway

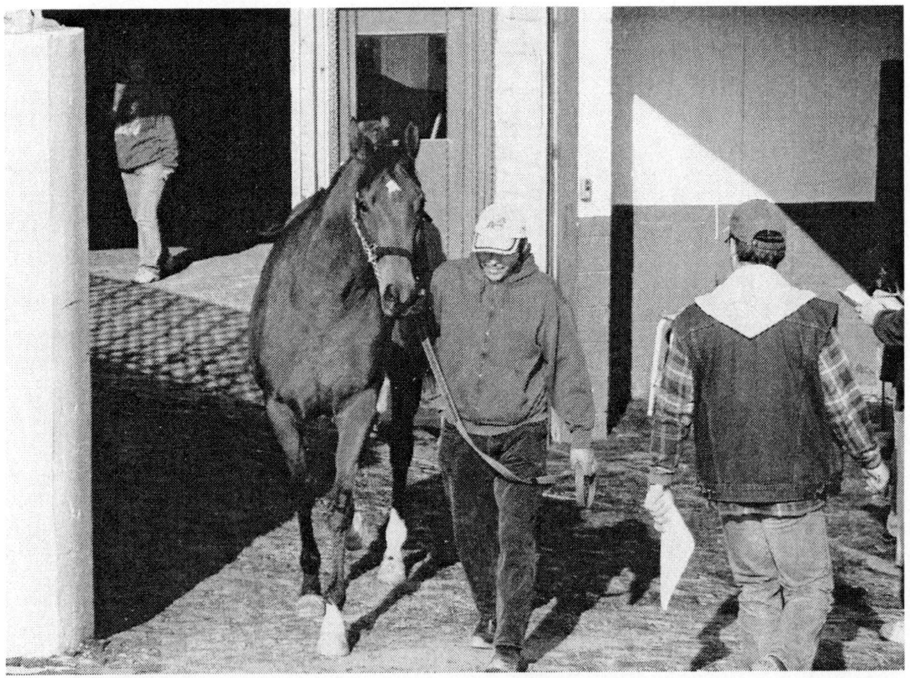

Hip number 1102 at the December 2005 Horses of Racing Age Sale conducted by Dan Arrigo, Buck's Pal was purchased by high bidder Dale Baird for $2,300. The horse had won one of 17 races in 2005, earning $11,320.

race in mind when he bid on the horse, and he was also planning to run in Fairmount's short sprints at low-level claiming prices.

Thinking with all the foresight and cunning of a chess master, Martinez had bought two horses at auction, both of which sold well below their depressed racing value. One of the horses was a router targeted for a specific race eight months in the future—a race not yet likely to be in any other trainer's thoughts—and the other purchase was a jackrabbit of a sprinter ready to deliver an instant return on investment. "Fusto and Dr. Robbie were the two horses I went to the sale for, and I was going to take them home no matter what I had to bid, within reason," said Martinez.

Dale Baird was high bidder on four horses at the auction, all of which would be vanned to Mountaineer. Like his younger counterpart, Baird had a plan for his new stock and expected that each of the acquisitions would be eventually adding to his world record win total.

At auction's end, Arrigo had produced a good show. The horses to be sold had been groomed to their best appearance; there was not a scruffy or used-up looking horse in the bunch, despite their pickle status. There were knee scars, high and low bows and other bumps and bruises documenting the physical traumas of a Thoroughbred's life on the track, but twenty-nine of the thirty-five horses had been sold for a total of $62,225, slightly above the $2,000 average required by Arrigo to break even.

The two-month layover period at Hawthorne between the end of the fall-winter racing meet and the beginning of the winter-spring dates is a time during which many horsemen take a deep breath and recharge. Most of the active horses on the grounds are kept in light training as weather permits, while the track-sore horses and competition-weary trainers nurse their physical and psychic wounds. A few horses occasionally ship the 300 miles south to Turfway for a race. By contrast, bloodstock agents such as Arrigo are in the midst of their busiest season due to the frequency and importance of auctions from October through February.

Less than two weeks after conducting the Hawthorne auction, Arrigo drove to Lexington, Kentucky, for the Keeneland Horses of All Ages sale, a more upscale counterpart to Arrigo's pickle auction. He worked the five-day duration of the sale, re-establishing contacts with potential buyers and sellers and making new acquaintances who showed potential or indicated interest. He also sold a handful of broodmare prospects he had collected during the previous six months and bought seven racing prospects for longtime friend and frequent client, Dale Baird. Purchases were also made for several other customers which included two just-turned yearlings. "The broodmare prospects I entered all sold well," said Arrigo. "It was a good, strong seller's sale and the margins my partners and I were able to get on what we sold were substantial. From a buyer's point-of-view, though, it was a tough sale. It seemed as though I must have been low or under-bidder on dozens of horses before I got anything. I was able to get only a very small percent of what I bid on. Sometimes the prices were just crazy. For example, a filly that had been claimed for a $10,000 tag on the West Coast sold for $35,000 as a *racing* prospect. Before the sale started I had talked with a consignor about a well-bred horse of his that I intended to bid on. He felt the horse was worth about $200,000, so I offered him $225,000 up-front, before the sale, if he would withdraw the filly. He wanted to take his chances in the sale, though, and wound up getting nearly $400,000 for her."

The day after the Keeneland sale ended, Arrigo drove to the Atlanta, Georgia, area to look at a horse he was considering for purchase. After rejecting the deal he deadheaded to Ocala, Florida, for the Ocala Breeders' Sales Company mixed sale from January 19 through the 22nd, buying four yearlings for various clients. From there it was a quick flight back to Chicago on the 23rd. On the 25th he packed up again and flew to Los Angeles for the Barrett's mixed sale in Pomona, California, where he bid just over $100,000 for a vanload of twelve horses of racing age for Baird. Once shipping arrangements were completed to van the horses 2,000 miles from California to West Virginia, Arrigo jetted back to Chicago. Two days after arriving back home Arrigo trailered Cart's Forty Four, trained by friend and barn neighbor Pam Little, to Turfway Park, where the horse was entered in a $7,500 claiming race. Two days later Arrigo and Cart's Forty Four returned to Hawthorne. The horse had won, but had not been claimed, and while in the area Arrigo had enjoyed a productive series of auction-related activities. He would now have several days' rest before the February sales started and the cycle was renewed.

"October through February are very busy auction months for

breeding and racing stock transactions," said Arrigo. "If a breeder buys a broodmare during that period he doesn't have to board her too long before it's time to breed her, which saves him some board bills. With a slackening in racetrack activity through the holidays the horses of all ages sales give depleted racing stables a chance to regroup and add some fresh stock."

Arrigo has made a living through the art of deal-making most his life; he thrives on the fast pace, quick-money turnover action and pressures of auction bidding and horse dealing, as well as with the burden of spending other people's money wisely. Long, stressful, and speculative hours are the norm: "Even in the summer when the sales market is slow I put in 13, 14 hours a day. My usual routine is to get up by 4 A.M., be at the stable by 5 and be done at the track by 7 A.M. By then I will have gone from barn to barn looking to buy or sell horses, and I normally would have completed any training necessary on the several horses I personally keep in training. Then, until early evening, I am either at the track or else spending much of the day in my office doing pedigree research, surfing the internet and doing phone work, laying the groundwork to buy or sell stock. I have to acquire horses in the off-season in order to have stock to sell at the winter auctions.

"Some people might consider it to be a hard life, but I wouldn't do anything else. I love it."

During a four-week period from late December through January, Baird had purchased horses at three different auctions, from Hawthorne in Illinois to Keeneland in Kentucky and on to Barrett's in California. For an investment totaling not quite $180,000 he had added 23 horses of racing age to his stable, freshening his stock and gearing up for another profitable run at Mountaineer purse money. The purchase price of the horses averaged a modest $7,800 despite the fact that most of the newcomers had well-established sires with five- and six-figure stud fees such as Rahy, Gentlemen, Seeking the Gold, Lear Fan, Red Ransom, and You and I in the first generation of their pedigrees. The broodmare sires of the fillies and mares included blue-chip studs such as Danzig, Woodman, Valid Appeal, Rainy Lake, and Lord at War. Other equine royalty such as Storm Cat, Deputy Minister, End Sweep, Talkin Man, Sir Cat, Marquetry, K.O. Punch, Spinning World, Key to the Mint, Fappiano, Groovy, and Caro (Ire.) appeared close-up in the pedigrees.

Paradoxically, pedigree means virtually nothing when buying older horses at auction, particularly males, or geldings, which are intended strictly for racing purposes. How the new horses would perform, or earn out, at Mountaineer Park is all that Baird cared about. The fillies and mares may have residual value as broodmares when their racing careers are over but Baird is an owner and a trainer, seldom a breeder. The object is to produce wins, not foals, and he wants purses, not promises. In his mind the practical value of his investment would play out over the next year or so on the racetrack, not in the breeding shed.

Baird's young counterpart, Ralph Martinez, was home in Collinsville, Illinois, spending the winter hiatus in his racing schedule by working the Shamrock Stable horses over the Fairmount Park track just regularly enough to maintain their conditioning. Occasionally an eager-to-run horse would be shipped a few hundred miles to Hawthorne or Turfway, but for most of the Shamrock Stable, including Martinez, it was a time to gear down. "We'll start the year at Fairmount and then go to Hoosier Park and end up the year at Turfway Park," explained Martinez. "We'll occasionally ship a horse to Indiana Downs, Hawthorne, Ellis Park and maybe a few other tracks, but our usual cycle is Fairmount-Hoosier-Turfway."

2

Lighting Up with a Loverboy

> *I like to have new owners in the game, but when somebody comes to me, the first thing I tell them is "You're not going to make any money. I hope I can help you break even and have some fun. Now, if that kind of a plan suits you, then [our farm] is for you, but if you don't like what I've just told you, then you'd better look for someone else to do business with. A lot of people think they're going to get in the game and make money...."*
>
> —Claiborne Farm's Seth Hancock in the January-February, 1995, issue of *Spur* magazine.

Give or take, it requires the better part of seven minutes for 625 crumpled up, used $100 bills to burn into unrecognizable rubble.... $62,500 reduced to a smoldering tray full of costly ashes that from physical appearances could just as well have been well-smoked

Cohibas as hundred-dollar bills. The actual incineration time on such a cache varies, depending on how tightly the bills are crumpled, whether the burning is conducted indoors or out (wind factor), and whether or not the fire-starter's hand is shaking as he puts match to gas or kerosene. A few years back, in 2000, two successful businessmen who had never met one another and who lived nearly a thousand miles apart partnered up and found that they had inadvertently discovered an even quicker way to burn up $62,500. They claimed a racehorse.

Call Me Loverboy was, in fact, just one of three Thoroughbreds claimed by Chicagoan George Getz and New Yorker Jay Petschek at Gulfstream Park racetrack, a major league winter spa for horseplayers in Hallandale, Florida, a few suburbs north of Miami. Petschek is a prominent investment portfolio manager imbedded in New York City's financial world, while Getz had shoved his University of Miami Law School degree to the rear of a sock drawer the day after he graduated. Forsaking a law career, Getz chose to pursue the life of a Thoroughbred breeder, owner and trainer in the Chicago area. His Nickels and Dimes Farm in Libertyville produced a number of good horses including Flag Officer, winner of the 1977 Illinois Derby, who was thought highly enough of to compete in that year's Kentucky Derby. Getz and Petschek, successful in disparate career paths, were unknown to one another but similarly were looking for some stimulating sporting diversion, and Thoroughbred racing seemed to have the answers. Coming to the same conclusions through different perspectives, Getz and Petschek anted up $200,000 to form J & J Stable (for Jay Petschek and George "Juddy" Getz).

The trainer they selected was wisecracking practitioner of all racetrack talents, Dan Arrigo.

A Chicagoan like Getz, having been born in nearby upscale Evanston, Arrigo was chosen by the J & J partnership as much because of his diverse Thoroughbred background and reputation as a no-nonsense square shooter as for his long, friendly relationship with Getz. In addition to maintaining a successful bloodstock business, Arrigo agreed to train for the new stable and to also serve as the point man in acquiring ready-made runners which theoretically possessed enough racing ability to ship north from Gulfstream Park to the prestigious Arlington Park meet later that spring. "I don't train horses to make a living," emphasized Arrigo. "It's a fun and challenging diversion," and few people in the sport have had as much fun as the multi-faceted Arrigo. In Getz and Petschek he found two kindred spirits who would give him a free hand in the training of J & J horses.

Getz would have trained the horses himself except for advanced Parkinson's disease, the debilatory effects of which had caused even the most routine of his activities to be significantly curtailed. No longer physically up to the rigors of full-time training and yet desirous of maintaining an active involvement in the sport, for several years Getz had relied on Arrigo for off-the-record advice and assistance. Petschek, who had previously been unknown to either Getz or Arrigo, had done some research on his own and learned of Arrigo's reputation for honesty and integrity in conjunction with his many previous successes as a syndicator, agent, buyer, seller and part-time trainer. "When I am asked for references," says Arrigo, "I just use two names: Dale Baird and Jack Van Berg, the two winningest trainers in history. Baird is number one in races won, Van Berg is second, and winning races is what horse racing is all about. In this business you want to deal with the organ grinder, not the monkey."

Those black-and-white references were good enough for Petschek. He wanted in on the action but knew he would be a hands-off partner. The financier/sportsman felt comfortable with the well-educated Getz and was equally confident that street-smart Arrigo was both knowledgeable and trustworthy. Between them, Petschek and Getz entrusted their new stable's trainer with the assignment of spending $200,000 for some fast-running, competitive stock that would, ideally, produce a favorable return on the investment, either through tangible purse winnings or, equally important, good times.

Aside from the fact that they had been total strangers, there was nothing unusual about Getz and Petschek's forming a modest stable of claiming horses. Approximately two-thirds of all races run in the United States are claiming races, contests in which the horses competing are eligible to be claimed, or are literally for sale. Horses change ownership in many of these races, and it is not unusual for a horse to be claimed several times throughout its career. Claiming a horse is a relatively low up-front cost entry into the sport, but with rare exception price tag horses have been tried on the track and come up a bit short of talent or speed. Occasionally such horses make their owners a profit, but usually not. Claiming horses is a bit like playing no-limit seven-card Texas Hold 'Em. Anyone can quickly learn the rules of the game but to excel at it takes experience, knowledge, patience, some luck, and nerves of tungsten. "Buyer beware" is the claiming credo as there is no obligation on the part of the connections of the horse entered to be claimed to explain why the animal is for sale. It may be that the horse simply isn't fast enough to compete against better allowance and stakes quality horses. It could well be that the horse has been injured in the past and his performance subsequently compromised. Or, it could be that the horse is ailing and the owners want to unload it while it still has some value, rather like trading in a car with a leaky transmission. It could be something as innocent as the fact that the horse no longer fits into the stable's plans and must be culled, either through a private sale or through a claiming race. The veteran Arrigo has been exposed to all the pitfalls of the claiming game and while he is widely recognized as one of the sport's most easygoing guys, he nonetheless has been able to make a substantial living for the better part of six decades by knowing when, why, and how to claim a horse, and for how much. He also knows when to sell a horse. Getz and Petschek had scored a bulls-eye with their selection of a trainer: the impish, good-humored track veteran had proved over and over that he is a guy you could trust with an unsecured six-figure investment.

The rules and regulations involved in claiming a horse vary slightly by racing jurisdiction, but the essence is that to claim a horse from a race (in other words, to buy the horse) you simply need to have enough funds on account with the appropriate department at the track to cover the cost of the claim, and you are required to have a licensed trainer, or agent, claim the horse for you. The process is not complicated. In Illinois, for example, a Claim Blank is filled out before the race, listing the track, the date, the name of the horse to be claimed, and routine information identifying the claimant. The form is then sealed in an envelope, time-stamped, and dropped into the claiming box no later than ten minutes before post time. The claim clerk then opens the box in private, checks with the bookkeeper to make certain that each of the claimants has enough funds in his horseman's account to cover the cost of the horse, and then checks the claim sheet to be certain that all details have been filled out precisely—even a slight misspelling will void the claim. A representative of each stable that has submitted a claim for that race is then summoned to meet with the claims clerk. If there is more than one claim entered for a particular horse, the clerk conducts a "shake," a lottery to determine who will be the winning claimant for the horse.

When a shake is required, the clerk puts the claim slips back into their respective envelopes, writes a number on the back of the envelope (1, 2, 3, 4, and 5, as necessary) and turns the envelope face down on his desk. Round plastic pills, each of which has one flat side with a number embossed on it corresponding to the number of envelopes, or claims, for a given horse, are dropped into a leather cup. The cup is then shaken and one of the pills is pulled from the cup. The envelope number that corresponds with the number on the pill is the winning claimant. Once the claimed horse leaves the gate at the start of the race he becomes the property of the new owner, for better or for worse, although any

ILLINOIS RACING BOARD **CLAIM BLANK**

Track: ______________________ Date: ______________________

I hereby claim the horse ______________________________ from the

________ race of this date, for the sum of $ ____________________ (Funds equal to or in excess of this amount have been credited to my account with the Horsemen's

STABLE NAME (If Applicable) ______________________________
(Print)

Name of Owner(s) ______________________________
(Print)

____

Name of Trainer ______________________________
(Print)

*Signature of Owner or Authorized Agent ______________________________

*SIGN IN THE SAME MANNER IN WHICH YOU SIGNED YOUR LICENSE APPLICATION

IL 579-0005

CLAIM

TIME

Please Stamp

______________________ TRACK

______________________ RACE

IL 579-0005

To claim, or buy, a horse from a claiming race, a card similar to the one shown must be filled out completely and accurately and dropped into a locked box at least ten minutes prior to the race. Claiming bargains are rare, but do occur. Seabiscuit ran in claiming races early in his career, as did Hall of Famer Stymie and 1999 Kentucky Derby winner Charismatic, among others.

purse money the horse may win from the race will be retained by the now-former owner. The horse can then be re-entered where the new owner pleases, depending on local restrictions applying to just-claimed horses, as long as the owner is duly licensed in the state in which he wants to run the horse.

Veteran trainer Ron Goodridge on claiming a horse: "Once we get the new horse back to the barn the first thing we do is to worm him and check his feet. Chances are, I am familiar with the training pattern of the trainer I claimed from, so I'll know how easy it might be to fit the horse into our regimen. All trainers have a regimen that they favor, but exceptions are made all the time. You can't always fit the horse to your system; sometimes you have to fit your system to the horse. Of course, maybe we don't try to do that. If the horse has been going good and has some peculiarities, we may just keep doing what has been done with him before.

"You can't always tell bows or other flaws, or potential problems, so we go over the horse real good, looking for anything we couldn't see earlier. You have to keep in mind that nearly all lower level claimers have something wrong with them. You just have to deal with whatever the problem is."

Bankrolled by J & J Stable money, Arrigo and his broad coterie of compatriots did the horseman's version of due diligence during the 2000 spring meet at Gulfstream Park. All Thoroughbreds racing within the desired price range established by J & J and Arrigo were studied for their action, or way of going over the track. Legs were given the fish eye for any signs of early or extreme wear and tear or unwanted lumps or bulges. Attitude, or desire, was evaluated as best as possible. Claiming price was contrasted with upside racing possibilities. The mantra of horse breeders everywhere—"Breed the best to the best and hope for the best"—wasn't a consideration because performance, not pedigree, is the only issue when claiming a racehorse. When claiming a filly or mare for breeding purposes, pedigree once again becomes a major factor in the claim.

I. At the Track

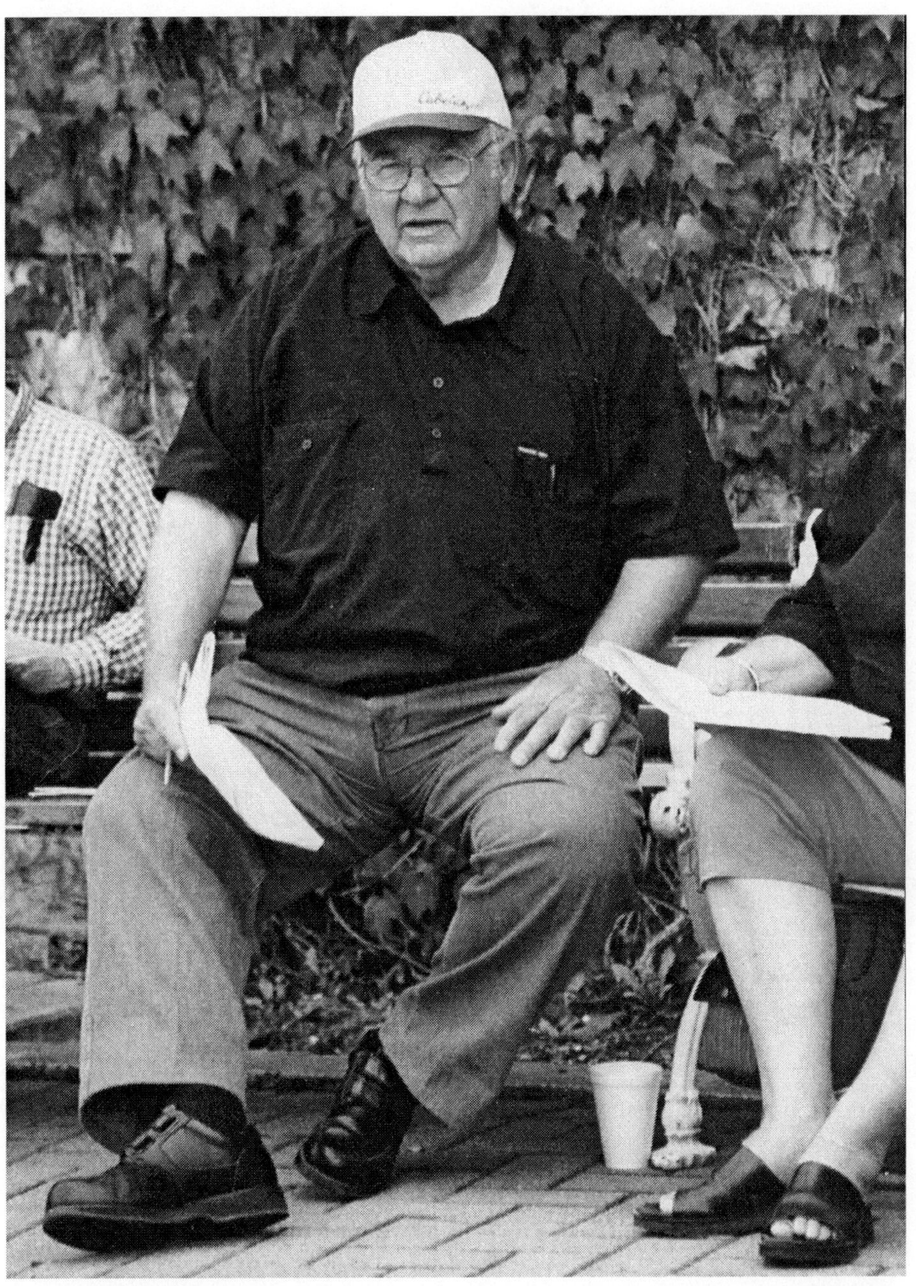

Eventually Arrigo and Robert Weiner, a free-spirited former Chicagoan who now functioned, among other things, as Arrigo's Florida-based freelance advisor, came up with several viable racing prospects for Getz and Petschek. The choices were narrowed to a handful of medium-to-high-priced claiming horses, but the look-at-*me* horse was a striking three-year-old lush mahogany bay by Gate Dancer out of Cupid's Way, by Lt. Stevens. The 16.2 hands Call Me Loverboy was an eyeful: well-developed with a strong, heavy-looking, opulent body constructed somewhere between the muscled look of a sprinter and the sleek grace of a router. He had a handsome, masculine head and a snakey blaze that dribbled from the center of his forehead down to his nose like a Jackson Pollock brush stroke. He showed a clear, intelligent eye and displayed just enough of a willful spirit to enlighten even a casual observer that he knew the difference between a saddle and a plow. Loverboy's sire, Gate Dancer, trained by Arrigo's friend Jack Van Berg, had nearly won the inaugural multi-million-dollar Breeders' Cup Classic in 1984. The horse finished second but was disqualified and placed third for his aggressiveness in a bumper car-type finish with two other horses. Earlier that same year Gate Dancer had won the classic Preakness Stakes in Maryland and followed up by winning the Super Derby

***Opposite*: Ron Goodridge is considered a claiming trainer, buying and selling Thoroughbreds from races in which each of the horses entered can be bought for a predetermined price. A claiming stable is in a constant state of flux due to the revolving-door possibility that a horse can be claimed—or a new one added—from any particular such race. But Goodridge also knows what to do with a top-class stakes horse when he gets his experienced hands on one. His most productive horse was a foal of 1990 named Brother Brown, who competed in high-level races from the age of two through four, winning 15 of 20 races while accumulating winnings of nearly $800,000. A precocious stakes winner at two, Brother Brown got his most noteworthy wins as a four-year-old when he won the 1994 Washington Park Handicap and the New Orleans Handicap, a race in which he bettered a thirty-year-old track record. Retired due to a race-related injury, the popular gelding now enjoys life as a pensioner on a farm near St. Louis.**

in Louisiana. Despite an outstanding race record, the Dancer was best known for his oddball apparel: he raced with ear muffs, a custom-sewn Bugs Bunny sort of headgear that fit over his ears to help block the crowd noise, although Arrigo used to tell Van Berg that the earmuffs helped the horse ignore the trainer's instructions.

Loverboy's dam, Cupid's Way, had also performed acceptably at the track, winning five of nineteen starts for earnings totaling $156,264, including a black type win in the Bouwerie Stakes at Aqueduct. Cupid's Way was the dam of nine foals, five of which were winners at the track, including the stakes-placed Empress of Love, who had won $220,153. Even without such a promising yet workmanlike pedigree, based solely on his general appearance and conformation Call Me Loverboy would have been the pick of the litter of most claiming trainers.

The good-looking horse didn't come cheap. Gulfstream Park is the sporting financial melting pot of winter racing, at least east of the Mississippi. High rollers from various racing sectors come south for the tropical climate, for fun and games, and they come with pockets full of discretionary dollars with which to frolic, gamble and claim horses. The ready availability of buying dollars creates an inflationary effect during the January-March Gulfstream meet. Horses are frequently entered to race for a higher claiming price than they would normally be priced at later in the year or at a different track. It is not uncommon to see a horse valued at a $20,000 claiming price at northern tracks running at Gulfstream for $30,000, and then, in order to be competitive, be dropped back to the lower price when racing elsewhere.

Call Me Loverboy had raced seven times before Arrigo dropped in a claim slip for him on February 3. The horse had made his debut the previous summer in a five-furlong maiden special weight race at stately Belmont Park in New York, finishing sixth, 9½ lengths behind the winner. He was then shipped to the more pedestrian Calder Race Track in Miami, where he placed second, seventh and ninth in three maiden races at six, six and seven furlongs. In each race he had run on or near the lead, and then backed up as he neared the finish line. Based on his abbreviated track record, his owner, Darren Jablow, was convinced that Loverboy needed to be dropped into claiming races in order to be competitive and to finally crack the winner's circle. The horse was entered in a five-and-a-half-furlong maiden claimer for $40,000 and finished an aggressive second, losing by a neck. Coming back three weeks later in a six-furlong $50,000 maiden claiming race on December 24th, he was sent off as the odds-on favorite, ninety cents to the dollar, and won off by 3¾ lengths under jockey Javier Castellano. The handsome bay was a maiden no longer and finished 1999 with one win and two seconds in seven starts for purse money totaling $19,460.

Taking advantage of Loverboy's good form, the horse's connections wheeled him back three weeks later at Gulfstream Park, which shares consecutive racing dates with Calder. A few miles but several cultures north of plebian Calder, Gulfstream is Florida's answer to posh Belmont Park or California's Santa Anita and attracts major stables, trainers and jockeys, all enjoying a combination business and pleasure respite. Starting the new year off on a positive note, Loverboy won a 6½-furlong $50,000 claiming race by a neck, coming from off the pace to win with authority. Maintaining the three-week race cycle, trainer Steve Standridge ran Loverboy back on February 3rd, although he was raised in class, or selling price, to $62,500. At odds of just above 5–1, Call Me Loverboy ran well for new jockey Richard Migliore, justifying the class boast by finishing second, 3¾ lengths behind the winner. The horse had posted two wins and two seconds in his four most recent races but he had run his last race carrying the Jablow silks.

The sharp-eyed Arrigo is near the point of the pyramid when it comes to evaluating racetrack talent, but the attributes that he and associate Bob Weiner saw in Call Me Loverboy were also apparent to other owners and trainers looking to acquire a horse in good form with upside potential. When the Jablow stable decided to continue to run Loverboy in claiming races despite the almost inevitable possibility of losing him via claim to another outfit, they did so without qualms. Jablow's operation was centered on allowance and stakes-class horses. A claiming horse, even a high-priced claimer who had as yet to peak, such as Call Me Loverboy, didn't fit into the stable's plans. When the horse was next entered, in a February 3 claiming race, there were seven claiming slips dropped in the claim box for him at the selling price of $62,500. The Arrigo-Getz-Petschek triumvirate would have to out shake six other stables in a roll of the flat-sided pills to determine who would have the right to lead Loverboy back to his new stall. There is usually not much strategy involved in shaking for a claim, but Getz had an angle. With his Parkinson's tremors becoming progressively worse, Getz said he would shake the cup of pills for his group. "You can bet," he said with gallows humor and trembling hands, "that nobody can outshake me." He was correct, and for $62,500 Call Me Loverboy became the property of J & J Stable, joining two other recently claimed horses to form the nexus of J & J.

With nearly two months left to run in the Gulfstream meet, Arrigo decided to race Loverboy several times before shipping north for the start of the Arlington meet in May. J & J kept the horse on a three-week cycle, running him February 26 in a six-furlong allowance race, which was a big step up in class. Loverboy was bumped at the start, shuffled to mid-pack and at the end of a minute and ten seconds he had finished seventh, beaten slightly more than seven lengths. It was not a bad showing considering the trouble he had at the start of the race combined with the fact he was facing a tougher group of horses than the claimers he had recently been running against.

Two weeks later Call Me Loverboy was entered in a mile and a sixteenth $80,000 claiming race on the grass, his first start on turf. Shane Sellers, at the time one of the leading jockeys in the country, was named to ride and the weekday betting crowd showed mild interest at about 7–1. When the gates clanged open Sellers had Loverboy away in good order, avoiding any repetition of the problems of his previous race. They were going well down the backside, but approaching the stretch turn the horse began to dramatically slow down. Sensing a problem, Sellers did not persevere with the horse. They finished in seventh place, beaten by more than thirteen lengths in 1:45.14. Worse, the hard-pounding bay had come out of the race gimpy. Bone chips were discovered in both knees. The damage was not life-threatening, but was career-threatening.

"You automatically assume the horse will be worth less when he returns to the track," said Arrigo. "The decision to be made was basically whether to remove the chips and bring him back to race at a reduced level of competition or to retire him. Loverboy was not gelded [castrated], so he could theoretically be used at stud but he hadn't accomplished near enough on the track to even remotely consider such an option. There are too many well-pedigreed stallions available which have proved themselves both on the track and in the breeding shed to keep a breeder from taking a chance with an ex-claimer with just two wins." If the horse were never to race again it would also mean that for their $62,500 investment J & J Stable had gotten about three minutes of race action ... roughly $21,000 a minute. Jay Petschek had taken bigger gambles before and would again: you don't get to be a successful Wall Street portfolio manager without a little educated risk taking. For his part, Juddy Getz had forsaken a career at law for a gambol on the track. He also knew risk. Dan Arrigo, a racetrack lifer, dealt with it every day. They analyzed their position, reviewed the options, and moved on accordingly. The three men all wore long pants; they knew there were no guarantees in life or in business, and certainly not at the racetrack. Having considered all scenarios, it was decided to remove the chips and to resume Loverboy's racing career if he came back sound—and fast—enough.

Even if the surgery and ensuing treatment were to prove successful, knee operations almost always have a negative effect on a racehorse's performance, in part because the knee joints are subject to calcification and eventual arthritis that could alter a horse's action and compromise his speed. The psychology of a serious injury is also an issue. The horse may intentionally slow himself up a bit—expend less than 100 percent of his energy—in order to avoid a recurrence of the problem and of the consequential pain.

"Older horses that have suffered a few injuries over the years learn how to take care of themselves on the track. That's how they get to be older horses," is a racetrack truism. However, when a Thoroughbred's racing ability is negatively affected even by fractions of a second he can drop from a stakes-quality horse down to a low-level claiming horse. In Loverboy's case, he had been a high-priced claimer with the potential to run in allowance or low-level stakes races. Post surgery, competing at that stratum was unlikely, although he could prove useful against lesser-quality horses. If it were possible to salvage Loverboy's career at the track, if he could be competitive at any level, he would still be able to accomplish much of what J & J Stable was looking for: racetrack action.

Two of the late aviation magnate Allen Paulson's horses provide a good example of how bone chips may or may not affect a horse. As a two-year-old, the European-trained Arazi capped a championship season by winning the million-dollar Breeders' Cup Juvenile stakes at Churchill Downs by more than four lengths in a manner that had railbirds recalling Secretariat. Less than a week after the race Arazi was operated on for bone chips in both of his knees, and while he was able to return to the track to compete in stakes races as a three-year-old, he never won another major event. Cigar, one of the greatest Thoroughbreds ever to step on a track, had bone chips arthroscopically removed from both knees in mid-career. The operation took an uneventful fifty minutes and the rest is history: Cigar went on to win 16 consecutive races while earning nearly $10 million. He was named Horse of the Year in 1995 and 1996. Giacomo, winner of the 2005 Kentucky Derby, is another example. After he competed in the third leg of the Triple Crown, the Belmont Stakes in New York, it was discovered that the big gray had bone chips in his left front ankle and his right knee. A routine two-hour operation was conducted to remove the chips with a full recovery forecast following a six-month rehab period. He did not return to the races in 2005.

The horse van originally scheduled to transport Loverboy from Gulfstream Park to Chicago's Arlington Park, normally a long but nonstop drive of 1,400 miles, made a detour en route north. Call Me Loverboy was dropped off at a state-of-the-art veterinary clinic in Ocala, smack in the middle of central Florida horse breeding country. Successful surgical procedures removed chips from both knees. Loverboy proved to be a good patient, and after a ninety-day rehab program at a nearby farm that involved extensive swimming (an exercise that kept weight off the restructured knees while allowing passive resistance conditioning), the big bay was back on a van to Chicago.

The ninety-day rehab program was followed by another three months of light on-track gallops and breezes. Finally, Loverboy was fit enough for competition. On September 3, six months since his last race, the J & J stable star was entered in a six-and-a-half furlong allowance race at Arlington Park. He would be running on the main, or dirt, track, Arrigo having abandoned the grass course experiment after one less than satisfactory result. Veteran Midwest jockey Randy Meier had Loverboy placed in mid-pack through the early stages of the comeback race: the rider was experienced enough to know not to ask the horse for too much too soon. By the time horse and jock reached mid-stretch, Loverboy began to noticeably tire, backing up to finish tenth, eighteen lengths behind the winner. His action, or leg movement while in full stride, had changed. It was not as fluid as before the surgeries. The horse was as determined as ever, but his feet hit the ground more with the authority of a jackhammer than with the grace of a cheetah, almost as though he were consciously making certain of every step, or stride. Loverboy cooled out uneventfully after the race except for a little post-surgery hitch in his walk that was more pronounced with fatigue. He ate up his evening meal with dispatch and showed no undue discomfort in the days immediately following the race. Arrigo continued with light fitness gallops in preparation for his next start.

The second test would come three weeks later in a six-furlong allowance race for a purse of $31,000. Meier took a return call to ride Loverboy despite the horse's bad beat three weeks prior. On a clear, sunny fall day Call Me Loverboy bounced around the paddock, snorting, flipping his mane about, showing he was eager to continue his comeback.

As soon as the gate sprang open Loverboy got into the bit, pulled Meier to the front and was running with the leaders until the stretch. Once again, however, the horse perceptively slowed through the final sixteenth of a mile—as though something was bothering him—and finished sixth, beaten over nine lengths. Confounding the good omens, Loverboy cooled out sore and a vet exam revealed the development of another knee chip. The damage was not life-threatening, and only one knee was affected, but it was again the perplexing type of injury that could end a Thoroughbred's career. After consulting with Petschek and Getz, Arrigo sent Loverboy back to the operating room where surgery once again proved successful. The patient was given ninety days of rest and post-op rehab, followed by three months of judicious, closely monitored training. Three scars, two on one knee, one on the other, plus a thumb-sized lump on the inside of his right knee, were visible souvenirs of the surgeries.

The handsomest horse on the track from the knees up was again ready for action.

3

Try, Try Again. And Again.

A self-sufficient, resourceful-by-necessity race tracker since his preteens, Dan Arrigo has learned to care about those who cannot take proper care of themselves. He heads up the local Horsemen Helping Horsemen fundraising efforts by conducting annual picnic atmosphere outings and raffles for needy track people, and it is not unusual on Friday mornings on the Arlington backstretch for Arrigo and fellow trainer Bettye Gabriel to cook up breakfast for anyone who has the time and need of a free meal. Such benefactions by Arrigo are not random soul-purifying acts of kindness, but a way of life.

A year and a day from the date his initial injuries were incurred, and six months from his second chip removal, Call Me Loverboy began comeback number two. The enforced inactivity had put the still-youthful and physically vigorous horse on edge, and he was as

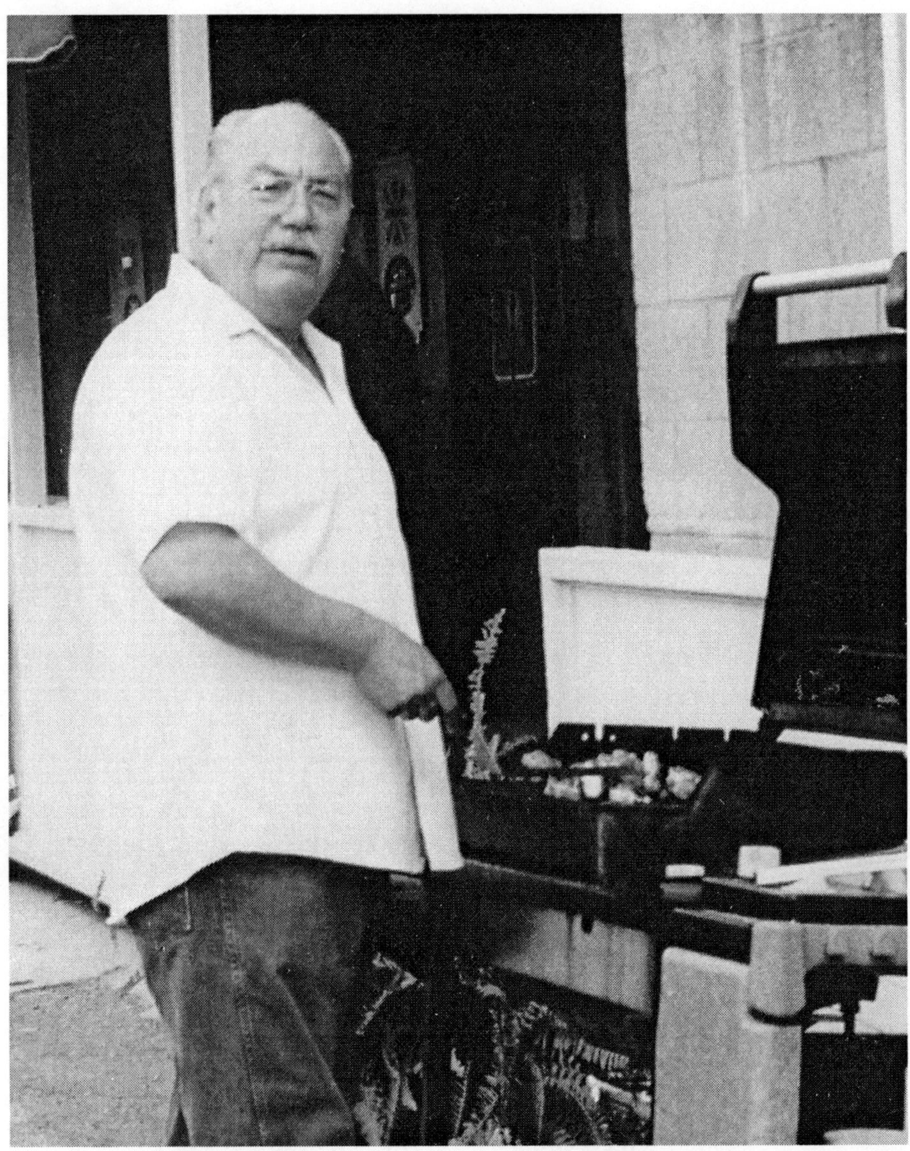

Dan Arrigo's insatiable appetite for track life has led him through a career as a gofer, hotwalker, groom, trainer, bloodstock agent and unofficial five-star benefactor chef.

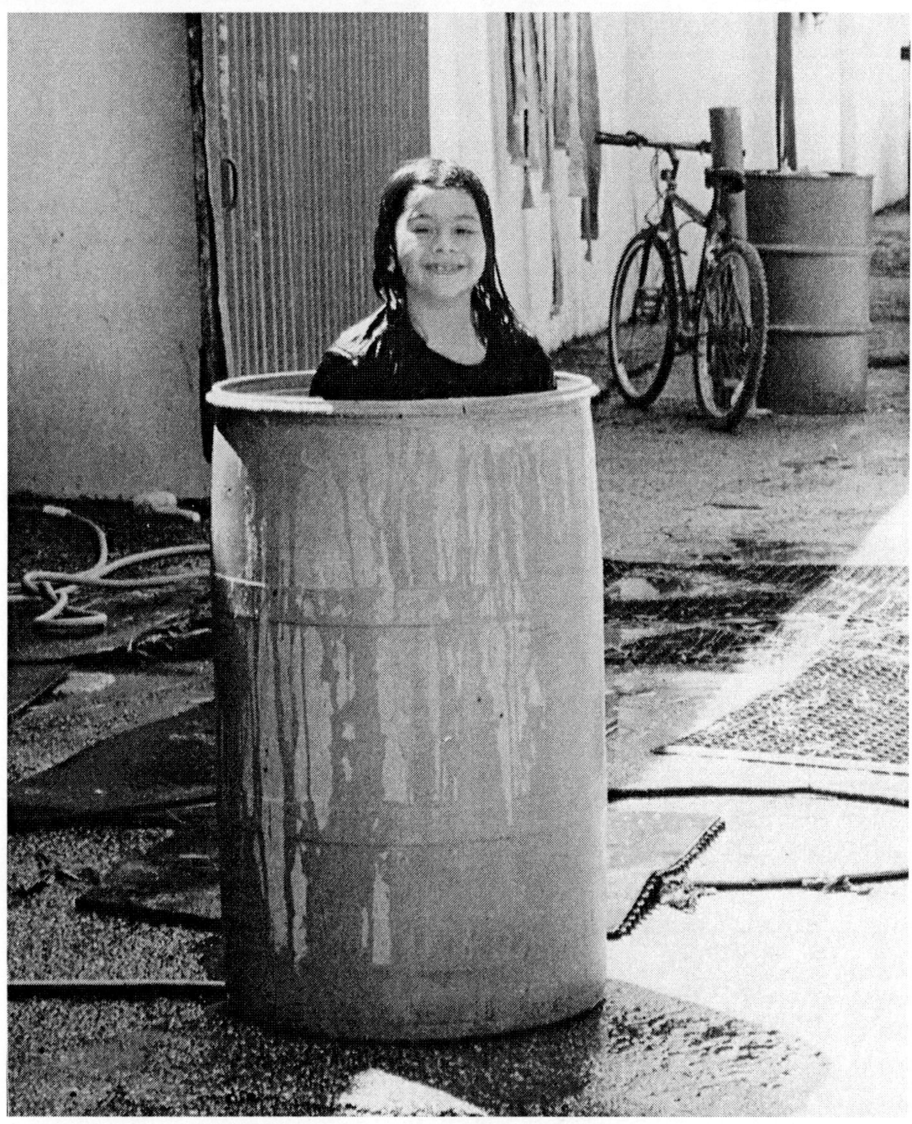

Amenities vary by racetrack, but above-ground pools, such as the one being enjoyed by Jacky Razo, are common at tracks that run during the hot summer months. Jacky's uncle Eddie was Call Me Loverboy's regular rider.

anxious for real competition as J & J Stable and Arrigo were to have him compete. "He's a tough horse to be around," said Arrigo. "He's not vicious, but he's rough in a playful way. He's well-mannered on the track, but around his stall he wants things his way. He's flipped grooms about, and if you are working on or around him he'll try to lay his weight on you. He'll sucker punch you with his muzzle when you relax around him, or he'll hit you with his shoulder or try to take a nip of you. But he's usually not the type of a horse that you get hurt around because he demands that you pay attention to him. Most accidents happen when a groom or trainer isn't paying attention to what they are doing near a horse." As luck would have it, Loverboy ironically required a lot of human interaction. "He's a high-maintenance horse, regularly running up a big vet bill and a lot of hands-on care. We stand him in a tub of ice for two hours in the morning, and then again for two hours in the afternoon, seven days a week. Loverboy is probably the only horse at the track that has his own ice-making machine."

In addition to bum legs, Call Me Loverboy had developed a serious bleeding problem that required ongoing care and attention, and was as perplexing an issue to deal with as the knee chips. Bleeding, or pulmonary hemorrhaging, in a Thoroughbred is usually a result of severe physical stress, such as racing or extraordinarily fast workouts. Commonly accepted treatment includes medication, usually the anti-bleeding diuretic Lasix (Salix), and lengthy rest. As part of the treatment, Loverboy's on-track conditioning work was conducted very early in the mornings while it was still dark because, according to Arrigo, "He's not as tough to handle in the dark as he is in broad daylight. He doesn't seem quite as confident, or get quite as stressed, galloping over the track before sunup. The less stress we put on him, the less likely we are to have a bleeding episode." From now on, Loverboy would be trained in near-darkness and would be placed in races at a distance and of a reduced competitive level that would tend to minimize the stress of racing to his lungs and knees.

The big bay had to date proved a costly investment. In addition to the $62,500 claiming price, the two surgeries added $5,000 to his tab. Additional costs included a year's training charges, miscellaneous ongoing vet fees and perpetual ice machine rental charges. J & J's total investment in Loverboy was nearing $100,000.

When Call Me Loverboy took to the track on March 9, 2001, he wasn't running at one of the premier tracks at which he had formerly raced, such as Gulfstream or Arlington. His latest comeback found him at the now-defunct Sportsman's Park, a ⅞-mile track that literally straddled the working-class communities of Cicero and Stickney, Illinois. Sportsman's was dead center in the middle of a gray, heavily industrialized smokestack area minutes from downtown Chicago and directly across the street from Chicago's other in-town track, Hawthorne Race Course. Sportsman's had a decades-long reputation of being a solid, working-guy bullring of a track that in previous incarnations had once hosted greyhound racing and enjoyed the patronage and benevolence of Al Capone. Now, the track was going through the death rattle of a failed experiment to convert to a multi-purpose sports facility: the plan had been to offer a Thoroughbred meet during the bad weather off months when Arlington Park or Hawthorne weren't running, and then—truth *can* be stranger than fiction—the dirt was scraped off the track to reveal, improbably, the Chicago Motor Speedway for open-wheeled Grand Prix circuit racers: the four-wheeled variety.

No matter where or what the venue, the fact that Call Me Loverboy had overcome serious obstacles ("I'd have placed the odds against him coming back at 99–1," said Arrigo, "but his owners were real sportsmen") to get back to the track was encouraging. The surgeries and conditioning regimen had proved successful to the extent that the big bay was able to lumber around the tight Sportsman's turns without incident in his first race back. He finished the six-furlong allowance sprint undamaged but uninspired, having run in mid-pack throughout. He finished seventh, eleven lengths behind the winner. For his effort Loverboy got a congratulatory pat on the rump and a few extra rations after cooling out. J & J Stable didn't collect a dime of the $29,000 purse, but despite the comments in the Equibase chart of the race indicating that Loverboy "showed little," Arrigo and J & J felt that there were some good races and payoffs left in the reassembled horse if he could stay sound. Allowance-level races were beyond Loverboy's capability now, and it would be necessary to place him at a reduced level of competition if he were to be competitive. For his next race Loverboy would run for a $25,000 claiming tag, the lowest level at which he had raced in his enigmatic fourteen-race career. "If we lose him, we lose him [to another trainer's claim]," shrugged Arrigo. "I don't want to raise him in class or run him too tough because of the problems he's had. I'm going to try to run him where he can win without overextending or hurting himself by breaking things loose. If I have to drop him down further, I will."

Five weeks later Call Me Loverboy ran fifth in a six-furlong $25,000 claiming race, earning $570 for his efforts. He ran a solid race, stalked the leaders throughout but weakened slightly in the stretch. Arrigo ran him back two weeks later in a $30,000 claiming race and Loverboy again put forth a good effort. He broke alertly under jockey Chris Valovich and ran near the front after the break, moved to second at the quarter pole and just lost the place position at the wire. His third-place finish added $2,640 to his earnings and helped materially validate the efforts to bring him back to the races in a racing-sound condition.

The handsome bay was beginning to be a money earner as opposed to a money burner, but the race was to be the last that Call Me Loverboy would run for Arrigo's friend and J & J Stable co-owner, George Getz, who succumbed to Parkinson's four weeks after the race. J & J now consisted of Jay Petschek and Arrigo, who assumed a partner's share in the stable in return for his services as trainer.

For what would be the final time in his career, Call Me Loverboy was taken out of the claiming ranks and entered into an allowance race on May 28 at Hawthorne. Going six-and-a-half furlongs, Loverboy—at odds of 28–1—broke slowly and was placed near the rear of the pack. He made a big move coming around the stretch turn to take the lead but again tired late, finishing fifth by 2½ lengths. Another $840 was deposited to his account, but more importantly, the race marked the beginning of a lengthy horse-and-jockey relationship.

Because of the pronounced hitch in his gait as a result of the knee surgeries, several jockeys had declined to ride Loverboy, sensing that he was unsound and prone to an on-track breakdown. When Arrigo offered the mount to Eusebio "Eddie" Razo, Jr., the veteran jockey had no qualms about accepting. Razo had been riding since he was fourteen, having begun his career in 1980 as an apprentice in his native Mexico. The young jock had proved to be a quick learner on a horse, and was helped along by tutoring from his father, who had also been a jockey and was now a successful trainer on the Chicago circuit. Razo, Jr.'s first win in the United States had come at Hawthorne in 1983, and by the time he swung a leg over Call Me Loverboy for the first time, Razo had racked up more than 1,500 wins. One of his most notable wins had been on Black Tie Affair in the 1989 Sheridan Stakes at Arlington Park, one of the races that helped propel him to Horse of the Year status. Razo felt that Call Me Loverboy was sound enough to race, and good enough to win a few more times. At the conclusion of the spring Hawthorne meet, Arrigo packed his gear and shipped twenty miles northwest to Arlington Park with the J & J Stable and several other horses. Razo wasn't available to ride for Arrigo during the Arlington meet, so first Zoe Cadman and then Valovich got the call. Loverboy ran competitively the balance of the year as Arrigo let him drift down the claiming scale. Loverboy initially ran for a $14,000 price tag, finishing seventh by eight lengths. After a two-month break to avoid the stressful summer heat that could prompt a bleeding episode, he was dropped into a $5,000 claimer, the bottom level at Arlington.

Ridden by Valovich, Loverboy finished second and earned $2,200 for his effort.

Shipped back to Hawthorne when the Arlington meet ended in September, Loverboy ran three more times before year's end. The races were at Hawthorne's lowest claiming level, $4,000, and the horse scored a fourth, a third, and a second-place finish in the three races, adding $3,515 to his cumulative earnings. Arrigo had found a level at which his patched-together warrior could compete with a realistic expectation of earning a paycheck. With Loverboy now in good form and racing competitively, there was the risk that Arrigo could lose the horse—J & J Stable's sole inventory—if a rival trainer claimed the big bay.

"Trainers see the horse is running good and maybe they get interested in dropping in a claim slip on him," said Arrigo, "until they check out the scars and lump on his knees and learn that we soak his legs in ice four hours a day, seven days a week. And outsiders don't realize that we spent $62,500 to develop a $5,000 claimer. At one time the stable may have had goals, or higher aspirations, for Loverboy. Now, my objective is to just get him around the track safely. Of course, it would be nice if he could pay for his upkeep, which is about $20,000–$22,000 a year."

Call Me Loverboy ran nine times in 2001, with a mixed report card. He had no wins, two seconds and two thirds for earnings of $9,765, incurring a net loss to the stable of about $13,000 for the year. On the plus side, his repair work stayed intact and it appeared as though he would now be able to deliver on the action that Petschek and his late partner, George Getz, had sought when forming the stable.

Loverboy made eight starts in 2002 ("His hole card seems to be lots of rest between races," said Arrigo), and the promise of the previous year came to pass, albeit modestly. In his first start of the year, March 17 at Sportsman's Park, Call Me Loverboy returned from a three-month layoff to end his 14-race losing streak, winning a five-and-a-half-furlong, $7,500 claiming race by a convincing three-and-a-half lengths. Regular rider Eddie Razo, Jr., rode him to the win and stayed on the horse throughout the year. The bay's first win in more than two years was worth $7,800, which would buy a lot of snow cones for the ice machine that was still cranking out the cubes being used daily on Loverboy's doctored knees and grumpy ankles.

The horse came back a month later and won again, topping a five-and-a-half-furlong $5,000 claiming race that added $7,200 to the J & J bank account. In two races Loverboy had scored two wins and added $15,000 in purse money. More significantly, Loverboy and Razo combined to formulate a new racing style. In his first race of the year, a more mature Loverboy had come from eighth place, well off the pace, to win. In his second race he had also come from behind, in seventh place, to score. Razo was now able to get Loverboy to rate, or to relax more at the beginning of his races, and then come with a swoop down the stretch. This more leisurely approach to the start of a race seemed to suit the horse just fine, reducing stress both on his legs and lungs. There would be no more bullet-from-the-gate, front-running starts for Call Me Loverboy. From now on, he would come from the back of the pack.

Aware that career-ending knee trouble was always just a misstep away, Arrigo scheduled Loverboy's starts far enough apart to give the horse ample time to recuperate from his races, but with two consecutive wins the trainer felt compelled to move him up in class. Arrigo upped him to a $10,000 claiming price and ran him three times throughout the next ninety days, once at Hawthorne and then twice at Arlington. The class increase proved to be too much as he finished 5th, 4th and 6th in three sprints, earning a total of $1,440. Dropped back to a $5,000 claiming price at the tail end of the Arlington meet, Loverboy finished a closing third. Finishing up the year in two subsequent races at Hawthorne, the big bay ran contentious races but could only finish 4th and 7th, signaling that it was time for a rest.

The ledger showed that Loverboy had scored two wins and a third in his eight races, good for $18,230 in earnings. His career earnings were at $68,915, which exceeded his $62,500 claiming price. However, $40,160 of his purse money had been won before J & J Stable claimed him. Loverboy had won $28,755 for J & J, not near enough to cover veterinary bills and training fees that likely exceeded his purchase price over the three-year period J & J had owned and raced him. The $62,500 capital expenditure, added to approximately $65,000 in operating costs, meant that the stable was operating in red ink, showing a loss of about $100,000 for the years 2000–2002. But the horse was still racing sound and his knees had held up against the rigors of a year-long campaign. Loverboy was running and winning, and providing action. And, knock wood, there would be next year.

After reviewing realistic options and prospects, J & J Stable stripped to the bare essentials for the new racing season. The two horses that had been a part of the three-horse package along with Loverboy when J & J was formed had been claimed away by other stables. "We got about what we had in 'em," said Arrigo with a whatta-ya-gonna-do shrug. "I don't remember the exact claiming prices." Racetrack wisdom, always selective, is to remember winners, not losers. J & J was down to one horse, and as the lone representative of the stable, Call Me Loverboy was to make six appearances in 2003.

Loverboy's final race of the previous year, over a semi-frozen track at Hawthorne, had been harder on his knees and ankles than first thought. He did not make his 2003 debut until May at Arlington Park, where he was entered in a six-furlong $5,000 claiming race. Eddie Razo again had the mount and would be his regular rider throughout the year. Responding favorably to the lengthy layoff, Call Me Loverboy broke tardily, languished near the back of the field down the backstretch and then responded to Razo's urging. Coming with a rush through the stretch, Loverboy finished a fast-closing second, missing the win by a neck.

It was nearly six weeks before Loverboy saw a starting gate again, running July 2 in a six-furlong, $5,000 claiming race. He again left the gate in a leisurely fashion and was 14½ lengths off the pace down the backstretch which, especially in a sprint race, is a lot of ground to have to make up. With horse and rider totally focused, Loverboy advanced to third at the top of the stretch and kept his momentum going, hitting the wire a neck in front of NobodyknowsbutEd. For his efforts in his first two starts of the year, Loverboy earned a total of $7,600.

Five weeks later Loverboy was in a $5,000 claiming race, once again at Arlington, but had to endure a rough trip. He broke slowly and, finding no holes or room to maneuver, he finished fifth, picking up $330. Chalk it up to one of those races where horse and jockey both tried, but the race just didn't play out favorably, which is particularly frustrating when the horse is racing on borrowed time and mended knees.

When Arlington Park closed for the season in late September, Arrigo maintained his Arlington-Hawthorne axis, shipping his one-horse stable to inner-city Hawthorne. On October 10, nearly sixty days after his previous eventful start, Call Me Loverboy won a six-and-a-half-furlong $5,000 claiming race by a length despite, or because of, being shuffled back to last at the break. The blood bay with the picturesque name and come-from-behind racing style was becoming a fan favorite among the hard core Betting People at Hawthorne.

For his last start of the year, on December 12, he was boosted in price to $8,000 in a six-furlong claiming race. The class hike proved a bit too much. Loverboy broke eighth, remained far back in the early running and was still just sixth at the top of Hawthorne's long stretch. He was only able to modestly improve his position through the stretch run, finishing a beaten fifth. The nearly frozen track had played extremely fast, evidenced by the fact that the winner's final time of 1:08.20—in a low-level claiming race—was just a hundredth of a second off the twenty-five-year-old track record (a record that would be broken two races later). Aside from being dragstrip fast, the track condition was unyielding and proved too jarring for Loverboy's knees. The effort of running such a fast time on the rock-hard track took a lot out of the horse; it was time to rest again. In fact, it would be nearly three months before Call Me Loverboy would do anything more serious than engage in leisurely gallops around the track on an every-other-day light training regimen.

Having been given ample time between starts to enable his throbbing knees, lungs and ankles to rest and recuperate, Call Me Loverboy had maximized his six race opportunities by winning three of the races, along with a second place and two fifth-place finishes. He earned a paycheck in every race and posted total yearly earnings of $22,105 ... just about the stable's break-even point for the high-maintenance horse. For his career, Loverboy now showed earnings of $91,020.

4

Rejuvenation, Risk, Reward and Retirement

Nobody's perfect. Acting as a middleman, Arrigo once bought a mare for Dale Baird—one of hundreds, perhaps thousands, purchased over a thirty-year period—that "didn't have a pimple on her, according to the seller. She had clean legs, was sound ... just a great-looking mare. I took the seller's word for her condition without actually seeing the horse, and had her vanned to Baird. He called me back the same day he got her. The mare was 100% sound, all right, but she was blind. Guess you could say I bought her sight unseen."

The mare, Street Smarts, was kept by Baird as a broodmare. She had two foals: the first ground out $38,000 in fifty-plus races; the other foal won $150, lifetime.

I. At the Track

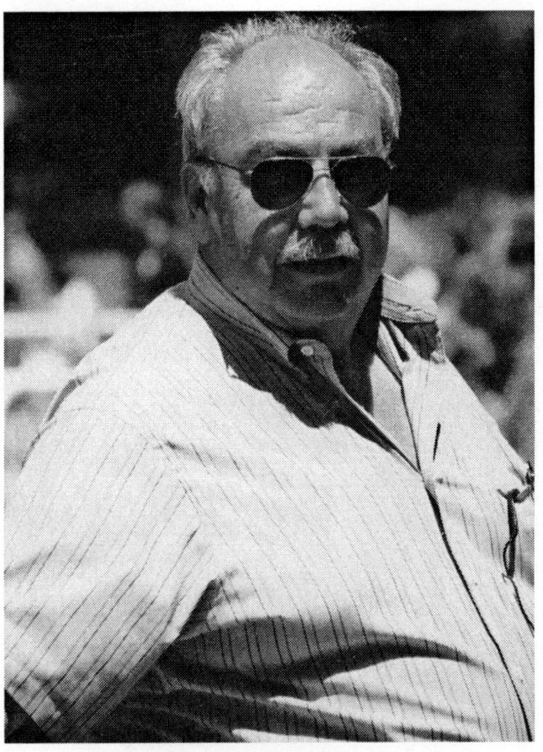

One of Dan Arrigo's rare miscues as a bloodstock agent involved the purchase of a horse named Street Smarts, who also should have been wearing dark glasses.

Spring brings with it rejuvenation, a freshening and revitalization more pronounced in northern climates where snow and slush turn into April showers; where brown landscapes turn to green; cold, blizzard winds become warm kite-flying gusts; and long sleeves morph into tank tops. The therapeutic wash of spring is especially welcome around the near-east side of Chicago, where inhabitants of stark Hawthorne Race Course seem to move about their business a bit more jaunty and where live racing becomes an option to smoky off-track betting parlors.

The winter had not been a good one for Call Me Loverboy, whose early spring was in danger of evolving into the late autumn of his career.

Because Loverboy had finished up the year in such good form, winning two of his last three races, Arrigo initially kept him in light training, using regular gallops to maintain his fitness as he followed another racetrack maxim: "Run 'em when they can go; lay 'em up when they get slow." Adage aside, it didn't take too long for Arrigo to realize that the particularly harsh Chicago winter weather was making even light training impractical for Loverboy.

The conditioning gallops over the unyielding, frozen track had caused the horse's feet, and then knees, and then eventually his entire body to sore up. Entered in a race at the end of the Hawthorne meet, Arrigo had to scratch Loverboy after the horse's halting action had telegraphed the obvious: he was neither ready nor able to race. A few weeks after the aborted start the trainer totally stopped galloping or working Loverboy, who was spending most of his time lying down in his stall to keep weight off throbbing knees and ankles. As a result, there was no way that the horse could be ready for the late February opening at Hawthorne. Of greater consequence was the fact that Arrigo had decided that if Loverboy couldn't physically come to hand by the end of the spring Hawthorne season he would discuss with partner Jay Petschek the likelihood of retiring the hard-trying but fragile horse. "If the track is okay I'm going to gallop him the last week in February and see how he comes out of the work. If he can handle the training, we'll go on with him. He's practically held together by glue, nails and screws, so anything we do with him will be day-to-day. I'll try to get him back to the track, but it's hit or miss. If he can't handle it we'll call it quits."

Before grungy, down-at-the-heels Waterford Park became born-again into glitzy, casino-supported Mountaineer Park, Dale Baird was well established as the "Wizard of Waterford" due in large part to the fact that he had led all North American trainers in wins for 15 years, racking up more wins than any other trainer in history, worldwide. Now, the "Master of Mountaineer," nearing seventy years old but still a fiery competitor, was having a difficult first quarter at the West Virginia track. From January through the end of March he had racked up just 12 wins from 143 starts, scoring at an atypical eight percent. While his $265,000 in purses led all trainers, he lost the first quarter training title, based on wins, to 32-year-old Scooter Davis. Scooter had 21 wins from 66 starts, a thirty-two percent win rate worth about $183,000.

Of the 23 horses Baird had bought through agent Arrigo at the

Hawthorne, Keeneland and Barrett auctions of horses of racing age, 11 had started a total of 15 times. The report card was not good: 0 wins, 4 seconds, 1 third, 4 fourth-place finishes. Ten of the races had been claimers, three were for maidens, and two were allowance races.

Baird was not particularly concerned; he could afford to be patient. He owned, outright or in partnership, nearly all of his horses, freeing him up from the aggravations of having to deal with owners pressing for immediate results, second-guessing him or waving condition books under his nose. Baird knew that some of the horses, especially those which were vanned cross-country from California as well as those shipping from Keeneland, would require a period of adjustment. The positive side, the silver lining, of the no wins from 15 starts meant that each of the new acquisitions had retained its "condition," or racing category. Maidens remained maidens, non-winners of two other than maiden or claiming could still compete at that low level, and so on. Because of the lucrative purse structure at Mountaineer most of the horses would only have to win one race to pay for their purchase price. Ideally, the horses would ultimately win and be elevated to the next condition, but in the meantime they were earning steady checks for second, third and fourth-place finishes.

To keep his stable fully stocked with ready to run Thoroughbreds, Baird purchases as many as 250 horses a year, usually selling off a similar number. In order to maintain an active and profitable stable of claiming and allowance horses (Baird has won more than $27 million in purses, much of which was accumulated at purse-poor Waterford Park), it is essential to constantly replenish stock that gets claimed, injured or retired. Knowing when to buy or sell makes a tangible difference to a stable's bottom line. By his own estimation approximately 99 percent of the horses Baird has owned or trained have been claiming horses, which means they more often than not required significant hands-on training and care to remain fit for racing. Despite the staggering number of horses that Baird acquires each year he seldom claims a horse, preferring instead to purchase privately. He employs bloodstock agents, or spotters, such as Arrigo to help him maintain an active stable that has averaged more than 1,200 starts a year since 1971—34 years and counting.

When Fairmount Park opened on March 26, young and energized Ralph Martinez had the huge, 95-horse Shamrock Stable cranked up, fresh from a three-month lay-up and ready to score. Ever since he had taken over the stable management from his father, Martinez had led the Fairmount trainer standings, and he got off to a good start in 2004 by winning four races on the opening card, including a five-furlong, $3,200 claiming race with Fusto, the recent Hawthorne paddock sale acquisition. A week later Martinez ran Fusto right back for the same price, at the same distance, and the horse scored a carbon-copy victory. Breaking alertly under jockey Ramsey Zimmerman, Fusto raced in second position down the backstretch, surged to a two-length lead at the top of the stretch and held on to win by slightly more than a length. In the three months since bidding $5,500 for the horse, Martinez had scored a second and two wins with the sprinter. Owner Louis O'Brien was financially "out" on the horse in that it had now earned more than the purchase price, but as is frequently the case with patched-up claiming horses, future plans had to be put on hold.

"He came out of his last race with a knee problem, so we'll lay him up until later in the year. We'll give him whatever time he needs," said Martinez, who had ample replacements to fill Fusto's spot on the stable's active roster. Since acquiring Fusto and Dr. Robbie at the Hawthorne sale, O'Brien had purchased an additional twenty horses during the first several months of the year to bulk up the stable. "Most of the horses we get are through private transactions, but we'll occasionally claim a horse, and every year Mr. O'Brien breeds a few horses from some of our better mares," explained Martinez.

Dr. Robbie, the seven-year-old chestnut gelding that had been beaten by more than 60 lengths in the two races prior to his sale to

Martinez, had responded well to a change in barns. "We don't have a set routine for new horses we bring into the stable," said Martinez. "We'll worm them, maybe give them Equipoise. Mostly it's just a case where we give them some rest and watch them closely to see what they might need."

Making his first start for the O'Brien-Martinez team on April 20—almost exactly four months since the paddock sale—Dr. Robbie responded well to the rehab program by finishing a closing second at Fairmount in a six-furlong, $5,000 claiming race. Ten days later, stretching out to a mile-and-70-yards claiming race at Indiana Downs, a distance that better suited his late running style, Dr. Robbie—as had Fusto—became a profitable acquisition for Shamrock Stable. The horse broke leisurely but alertly, took the lead at the three-quarter pole and held on to win by a diminishing head. A month later Dr. Robbie ran again at Indiana Downs, going 1⅛ miles for a $7,000 claiming tag. He broke near the front of the six-horse field, fought off two challengers pressing him for the lead, and won by a neck. His first three races for O'Brien-Martinez had produced a total of $11,420—$9,120 more than his $2,300 purchase price. The trainer was pleased with the early results. "He's turned out to be a real bargain, and I don't want to lose him before the Ellis marathon series. We won't run him for a claiming price anytime soon." Martinez had the horse going good and in a competitive frame of mind. "He has been feeling so full of himself that the day before his win at Hoosier Park he had run off with the exercise boy and galloped two miles around the track before we could pull him up. He's one tough horse. I'm not surprised he put together back-to-back wins."

There was no doubt that Dr. Robbie would be ready for the marathon races later in the summer, the stakes series for former low-level claiming horses that Martinez had in mind when he shouted out the high bid on Robbie four months earlier.

When Call Me Loverboy returned to the barn with his ears pricked and his neck bowed after breezing three-eighths of a mile in :38.20 over the mellowing Hawthorne track toward the end of March, it was as though the ache in his knees had evaporated along with the snow and ice of winter. Eulogio Quinones, who had been galloping and working Loverboy for more than three years, knew all the physical and mental nuances of the horse, and the usually laconic Mexican had a wide smile on his face as he slid the tack off the bay's broad back. "He's feeling good," he told Arrigo. "He's starting to stretch out better. Longer stride, not such a choppy motion."

Quinones is uniquely qualified to assess the pieced-together horse's frame of mind and physical condition. Tall and heavy for a gallop boy, standing about 5'9" and weighing at least twenty pounds more than the average exercise rider, Quinones is too heavy to gallop most horses. He subsidizes his wages as a groom and part-time gallop boy by doing farrier work, and has served as a veterinarian's assistant. He can detect a foot problem within a stride or so, and his veterinary experience has served Loverboy well. Quinones' weight is not a factor when working Loverboy because the horse's above-average broad girth and weight enable him to carry Quinone's extra heft without undue strain.

With Loverboy doing better, Arrigo felt safe in increasing his on-track activities. Every day the horse was taken out of his stall to engage in some form of training activity: galloping, jogging, breezing, or simply walking about the shedrow ... whatever Arrigo and Quinones felt the horse was capable of on that particular morning. By the end of March Loverboy had posted three official works in addition to several training outings that were considered too slow by the clockers—the sharp-eyed racetrackers who have the responsibility of officially timing the training efforts of each horse with a stopwatch—to be registered as timed workouts. Arrigo could see the horse was on edge, ready for a race, and as he flipped through the pages of the condition book (issued by the track every several weeks, it lists the upcoming races and what the conditions, or qualifying factors, are for each race), the trainer found a six-furlong claiming race on April 2 that was a good fit. The race was for horses entered to be claimed for $6,000 down to $5,000, with weight concessions based on past performances. Call Me Loverboy would be assigned 118 pounds including the jockey and tack. The weight would seem like a feather to the horse, which was used to carrying the burly Quinones in his morning workouts.

On Monday morning, March 29, the day after Loverboy's encouraging work and just minutes before the 10:00 A.M. entry deadline, Arrigo, bothered by the lingering effects of gout, limped into the racing secretary's office and formally entered Call Me Loverboy for the April 2nd race. If there was no rain in the interim, or any other unplanned incident, the horse would run. "He coughed once this week," said Arrigo, "but that shouldn't bother him. He runs his eyeballs out when he's fresh, so I expect him to run well after a three-and-a-half-month break. The $6,000 claiming price is the right class for him. Too bad it took us $62,500 to find that out...."

Even without the stable's bright red horse blanket and neon-yellow blinkers, Call Me Loverboy would have been easy to spot walking from the stable to the paddock on race day. Physically imposing due to his height and girth, he held his head level as he walked at a haughty, measured pace as though en route to his coronation. His limp was barely noticeable; he was not to be hurried. This was the 36th time Loverboy had entered a paddock to be tacked up for a race: the racehorse knew what was expected of him, and he appeared ready and able to deliver.

In fact, Loverboy felt much better than his trainer, as Arrigo was still hobbling around on crutches, aching from the renewed gout attack. "Between the two of us," Arrigo winced, "we don't have two good legs, let alone six." With Arrigo semi-incapacitated, Pattie Miller, wife of trainer Danny Miller, saddled Loverboy in the paddock, smoothing the saddlecloth over Loverboy's back, centering the saddle on the cloth and then tightening the girth. Regular jockey Eddie Razo, Jr., walked up to Arrigo in the stall to get any last-minute instructions. Razo had been on the horse enough that he didn't need tactical advice, but Arrigo wanted Razo to look out for any signs of ill effects from the long winter layoff. "We'll find out soon enough," said the jock with a shrug as he was given a leg up on the horse. Horse and trainer limped out of Hawthorne's indoor paddock into a bright, clear 50° day. "Perfect day for a race. No excuses today," said Arrigo, giving his horse a parting slap on the rump.

Razo warmed up Loverboy slowly. After an almost casual muscle-stretching gallop following the post parade, the horse nonchalantly walked the remaining half-mile to the backstretch and to the starting gate. Eight horses were entered with eight-year-old Be Valiant a slight 2–1 betting favorite. By Lord Avie out of a Danzig mare, Be Valiant had what is called "back class," meaning that earlier in his career he had run in events of more significant stature than the current $6,000 Friday afternoon claiming race. He had, actually, raced 60 times, with 8 wins and nearly a quarter of a million dollars in earnings to his credit. Call Me Loverboy, however, showed excellent recent form, having won two of his last three races. Additionally, he was dropping from an $8,000 claiming race to the $6,000 level. Loverboy was the second choice of The Betting People at 5–2.

The horses were all veterans and loaded into the starting gate without incident. Starter William Knott sprang open the doors on schedule at 4:27. It was a clean start for all, with Loverboy and Rivets dropping to the rear as first Toast the Host and then Cuban Leaf battled for the early lead. Call Me Loverboy was sixth down the backstretch and into the top of the stretch, while Good Better Best wrested the lead from Toast the Host. At 1,320 feet, the Hawthorne stretch is one of the longest in the country, and as Razo shook the reins at Loverboy, communicating that it was time to accelerate, the horse energetically responded. He began narrowing the gap between himself and the lead horse, powering down the lengthy stretch, oblivious to any ancient injuries or damage, the track a canvas for his grace and athletic artistry. "He is an older horse; he knows what to do," Razo would say after the race. "He's a very willing horse. I didn't have to use the whip to get him going." By mid-stretch Good Better Best still had a slight lead, but Toast the Host was moving up along the rail and Be Valiant was charging down the middle of the track, both horses in single-minded pursuit of the leader. Coming fastest of all, however, was the big bay with the neon-green J & J blinkers, Call Me Loverboy. Barreling along the outside as though shot from a circus cannon, Loverboy passed them all, crossing the finish line a length clear of runner-up Toast the Host. Be Valiant finished third.

The time of the race was 1:12.4, much slower than the 1:08.21 of his previous race nearly four months ago that was run over a frozen track. The surface was deeper for today's race, and much easier on Loverboy's legs. As he confidently pranced back to the winner's circle with a zest that belied his seven years and numerous infirmities, Loverboy was barely puffing. His mouth was closed and he held his head upright and steady, showing no indication of pain. The only tell-tale signs that he had been in a race were his forelock, matted down with sweat, and the front half of his body, which was coated with track dirt, transposing him from a dark bay to a light brown sand color. It was the third time in his last four races that Loverboy had gone to the winner's circle to get his picture taken. The horse stood statuesque, ears pricked, as Arrigo balanced carefully on his crutches and cell-phoned the welcome result to co-owner Jay Petschek.

After unsaddling, Eddie Razo told Arrigo what the trainer had hoped to hear: "The horse was as good as he was before the winter layoff." There had been no claim slip entered for Call Me Loverboy; he would be going back to his familiar stall in Barn 2B after a stop in the Detention Barn for routine but mandatory drug analysis tests.

There is nothing physically attractive about Hawthorne's Detention Barn. It's a brick, oblong-shaped, near-windowless building that from the outside looks more like a nearby Cicero Avenue auto chop shop than a horse barn, but it is one of the most popular buildings on the grounds. Located along the backstretch about a ten-minute walk from the winner's circle, the barn is where every owner, trainer and horse wants to hang out after the finish of a race because that's where the winner is required to go for drug testing.

After entering the Detention Barn the race winner is methodically cooled out while waiting to give a blood and urine sample, being slowly led in circles around the interior perimeter of the barn by a groom who rarely shows the same flush of excitement as the winner's connections. After ten or fifteen minutes the horse is led into a closed-off stall and encouraged to pee into a metal cup. "Three things you don't want a horse to do to you," says Arrigo. "You don't want to be kicked; you don't want to be bit; and you don't *ever* want to be pissed on. That's why there is a two-foot-long handle on the pee cup." The official in charge of securing the sample has some sort of politically correct job title, but horsemen simply call him the piss collector. The collector encourages the horse to urinate with dispatch by softly whistling to him and rustling the bed of straw covering the stall door. Once the horse relieves itself, the sample is taken to laboratory-type offices on the opposite side of the walking ring where two split samples are secured into sealed cups for analysis. The horse is then walked a few more minutes until he is completely cooled out, at which time a state veterinary official takes a blood sample which is then sent off-premises for sophisticated drug testing.

Call Me Loverboy circled the rubberized Detention Barn walking ring with a bright, inquiring look, as fresh as a two-year-old. His eyes were alert and his ears were pricked. Each trip around the walking ring he would glance sidelong at Arrigo as though looking for affirmation of a job well done. The horse had coughed twice on his way to the barn, and though coughing after a race can be a sign that the horse had bled, in this case it was more likely a result of Loverboy's having swallowed racetrack grit during his come-from-behind romp. Otherwise the big horse showed no signs of fatigue, but that would likely come later; body and leg soreness, if any, would not set in until the day after the race.

I. At the Track

Even though Arrigo had owned and trained horses for years and was a high win percentage trainer, and even though Loverboy had merely won a low-level claiming race, the trainer was pleased. Objectively, it could be more difficult to get a sore-legged horse ready to run for a tag than to get a sleek three-year-old stakes horse ready for a Grade 1. "Tomorrow morning is fiesta time around the barn. I'll bring tacos and tamales for the barn crew," he said.

The eighth race at Hawthorne Race Course on Friday, April 2nd, was in the books. Call Me Loverboy had paid $7.40 to win, $3.80 to place, and $2.60 to show. The 7–2 exacta paid $30.40; the 7–2–3 trifecta paid $69.60; and a $2 superfecta of 7–2–3–6 paid off $428.20. Some of The Betting People sauntered to the windows to cash in: most just turned the page on their simulcast program to the 9th race, an allowance for Illinois-breds.

Several hours after the race it seemed as though Loverboy had come through his effort in good order. He devoured everything in his feed tub and was plucking at the hay rack hanging just outside his stall door. The following day he was given his full ration of feed and ate hearty. "We give him three meals a day," explained Arrigo. "He's a big, stout horse with a huge appetite. He is fed two quarts of oats for his 4:30 A.M. breakfast, and at 10:30 A.M. he gets another two quarts of oats, a quarter scoop of sweet feed (a combination of oats, barley, corn, molasses and trace minerals) to make the feed interesting. At 4:30 P.M. we feed him four more quarts of oats, two quarts of sweet feed and two quarts of bran. Overall, he gets about twelve quarts a day, which is a lot of feed. That doesn't include vitamins (at $60 a gallon), k.c. powder, thyroid medicine, and electrolyte granules."

Two days after his race Loverboy seemed ready to get back to the track. "He is really feeling good, both mentally and physically," said the trainer. "He's acting fresh and is anxious to gallop. I wish his knees and legs were as sound as his head. He's got a couple of little nagging things I'm watching, but he could possibly be ready to run before the end of the meet. The problem is, if I run him again near the end of the Hawthorne meet he could be claimed and then shipped downstate to Fairmount, or elsewhere. If I wait to run him at Arlington and he were to get claimed, the new owners wouldn't be able to ship him off-track for nearly a month ... which might cause them not to drop in a claim." Not being able to relocate the horse to a more advantageous track could be a deterrent to his being claimed, and Arrigo was not anxious to have the productive half of his two-horse stable claimed after nursing him through wins in three of his last four races.

Less than a week later things changed dramatically for J & J Stable and Call Me Loverboy. The horse was gimpy again, body and leg-sore, too achy to go to the track, too sore to even stand in his stall for any length of time, according to Arrigo. "It seems to be a recurrence of old injuries and problems. We x-rayed him this morning to see what damage, if any, had occurred during his last race or since, but he may be through no matter what the x-rays show. I'll rest him through the early part of Arlington and see how he responds to light training. Otherwise, I know of a riding farm in Wisconsin that's looking for a stud horse, and I may send him there."

Waiting for the Hawthorne meet to wind down and as a preliminary to the late spring startup at Arlington Park, Arrigo kept busy buying and selling racing and breeding stock. Within a 30-day period he bought and sold more than 50 horses, most of which would be considered pickles. With the breeding season nearly over, a number of the newly acquired mares were immediately shipped to Kentucky farms to be bred, while the rest of the stock went to different stables at various tracks in an attempt to maximize the earning power of the horses. One of the 50 horses that found a new home was Conngent, a maiden gelding owned by Hawthorne management that represented half of Arrigo's stable. The horse had gone through a series of ligament and other assorted leg problems, and a pulled hind tendon confirmed that the injury-prone horse could no longer stand training. From now on, Conngent would spend his time as a riding horse on a farm in northern Illinois.

On May 14 the spring/summer Arlington Park meet opened, and Arrigo transferred his one-horse stable to Barn 5, Stall 96, on the Arlington backstretch. The twenty-mile van ride from Hawthorne to Arlington had been uneventful, and Call Me Loverboy was soon comfortable in his new, low-key routine. His front legs were regularly painted with a white poultice and swathed in leg wraps and he continued to stand with his front legs in a tub of ice four hours a day. Even though his exercise was limited to two daily walks around the stable area, his attitude was good, even playful. When a groom or visitor would try to ignore him he would grab at their arms, jacket or anything within reach to get attention, or to mooch a treat. Responding to the crackly unwrapping of a hard mint, his ears would prick and his head would bob, his black forelock dropping seductively over his eyes. He would do this, bobbing his head first up and down and then sideways, until he was given a treat. Soft, rubbery lips would gently scoop the mint from the flat of an outstretched hand, and after a few thorough crunches the head bobbing and nipping would start again. But Call Me Loverboy's outward bonhomie belied deeper problems.

"He's through," said Arrigo in mid–July. "He's had enough racing. He just takes too long to get sound between starts. He's seven, and all the injuries and problems have caught up with him. I don't want to chance him snapping off a leg. He's got three bad legs and heat in his ankles. There's a farm in Mexico that's actually interested in standing him at stud, and I've got a few other options if that doesn't pan out. But he's done racing."

Call Me Loverboy retired with eight wins from 36 starts, and earnings of $97,920. He went out a winner, having won three of his last four starts, including his final race. J & J Stable lost a significant portion of their investment but had a good run, claiming a few horses, getting some wins. Now, the horses were gone and the stable barn door literally closed. Except as a paper technicality, J & J ceased to exist. Because Call Me Loverboy was not a high-profile stakes performer, far from being a marquee horse, no announcement of his retirement would be forthcoming. He simply would no longer appear in the *Daily Racing Form* as a handicapping option for the Betting People.

5

A Time of Reckoning

It had been a defining year for Call Me Loverboy. On the one occasion when he was sound enough and fit enough to compete, the horse showed on the track the potential he possessed before injuries compromised his performance level. It was a happy ending as Loverboy left racing a winner, and his trainer was eventually able to find a home for the horse outside of racing. Arrigo, for the short term, would walk away from training to concentrate on his bloodstock business.

Dr. Robbie, Fusto, Dale Baird and Ralph Martinez had also been through watershed years, to mixed effect.

It was Dr. Robbie, the inexpensive club-footed auction pickle that trainer Martinez had nurtured into a consistent winner, that experienced the most dramatic highs and lows. Robbie's first three races for Martinez and the Shamrock Stable had been in claiming races, progressively escalating from $5,200 to $7,500 and finally to

$9,800. He finished second in his first race for the stable, a six-furlong race on April 20 at Fairmount Park, and then—once stretched to a mile or more—won his next two starts, both at Indiana Downs. Returned to Fairmount for a starter handicap race at a mile-and-a-quarter on July 3, Robbie ran away from the field, galloping through the stretch to win by nearly seven lengths under jockey Ramsey Zimmerman, a transplanted Chicago jockey who rode first call for Shamrock.

Just prior to the starter allowance series of stakes races at Ellis Park that would culminate in a $25,000 marathon stakes event, the races for which Dr. Robbie had been primed from his first day in the stable, Martinez had to revise his game plan. Ellis had modified the eligibility rules for the starter marathon series, making the races open to horses that had run at Ellis for any claiming price. Theoretically a horse that had run for a $100,000 price could enter and totally dominate horses that had been running for $10,000 or less, such as Dr. Robbie.

To expect Robbie, who had run in claiming races for a value as low as $4,000, to compete against horses which had run in claiming races of $50,000 or even more was unrealistic. Martinez set aside the marathon racing series plan and looked for softer pickings. A nine-furlong starter allowance race at Ellis Park at the end of July seemed to be Robbie's for the taking, and the Betting People thought so, too, sending him off at 3–1 odds. The van ride from Fairmount to Ellis had apparently been hard on Robbie, however; the midsummer temperature reached nearly 100°. When it came to race time, the chestnut gelding's strength had been sapped. Tiring through the stretch, he finished tenth, beaten nearly eighteen lengths.

A post-race veterinary exam didn't reveal a cause for the disappointing performance except possibly fatigue brought on by a combination of the van ride, the heat, and the race. Returned to Fairmount Park and entered in a one-mile $10,000 optional claiming/allowance race three weeks later, Dr. Robbie broke well but had to check, disrupting his momentum soon after leaving the gate. Despite the interference he rallied to finish a fast-closing second, beaten by a photo-finish neck.

The race served to reassure Martinez that there was nothing serious troubling Robbie. The trainer ran him back eight days later in a similar race, also at Fairmount, in order to avoid shipping in the heat. This time Robbie enjoyed a trouble-free trip. Ridden by Ramsey Zimmerman, the horse broke in mid-pack over a muddy track, held his position through the backstretch and then charged home through the stretch to win going away by two lengths at odds of less than 2–1.

The Fairmount condition book was running out of non-claiming races for Dr. Robbie, who had registered two wins and two seconds in four starts over the Collinsville, Illinois, track. Indiana Downs in Shelbyville, Indiana, was a marginally shorter van ride than Ellis Park, approximately four hours, and the track had a race scheduled for September 8 that suited Robbie: a flat mile for a $10,000 claiming tag. The horse was familiar with the Indiana track, having run there two years previously when he had won two of three starts, and was third in the other. The Hoosier Betting People were wise enough to know that the horse had been through considerable wear and tear since he had last raced at their track, but nonetheless noted his present good form and sent him off as the odds-on favorite at 4–5. With Zimmerman up, Robbie broke well but was unable to save ground, being forced to run four wide most of the race. He tired through the stretch and finished fifth, beaten nearly nineteen lengths. He had not performed with the expectations of an odds-on favorite, and Martinez again had him thoroughly scoped and checked out, to no avail. Unless he had simply developed an aversion to shipping even short distances, whatever was troubling Dr. Robbie was not evident to the trainer or his vet. Two days later, Dr. Robbie collapsed in his stall, dead of a heart attack.

"It's just a shame," said a somber Martinez. "I wasn't in the barn when it happened but my vet called me right away. Said Dr.

Robbie just keeled over and was dead in thirty seconds. He was a good horse, had a great personality. He would mess with you, playfully bite at your arm or whatever, but he never tried to hurt anybody. Just a shame...."

Dr. Robbie ran seventy-six times, age two through seven, with eighteen wins, fifteen seconds and seven third-place finishes for total earnings of $196,869. Running in the Shamrock Stable colors, Robbie had run eight times from April through September, with four wins and nearly $25,000 in purse money.

The success Martinez had with Fusto, the speedball claimer he bought at the same paddock sale at which he was high bidder for Dr. Robbie, was less bittersweet.

"We knew Fusto had a knee problem and would require special handling when we got him," said Martinez. "But he can deal with shorter distances without too much trouble. We run him a few days after we bought him and he come in second by a head going five furlongs on a muddy, tiring track at Turfway. We run him back twice at Fairmount at five furlongs for a $3,500 claiming tag and he win both times. A horse like Fusto, though, you can only run so many times and then you have to give 'em a rest. After his second win at Fairmount, in April, we laid him up until September when we brought him back going six furlongs at Hoosier Park. Six furlongs is like a marathon to him, though, and he tired pretty badly. He'll win next out when we find a five-furlong race for him."

For the year Fusto had raced four times, with two wins and a second good for $6,340. Combined, Dr. Robbie and Fusto had won $31,154, a positive return on their joint purchase price of $7,800.

Louis O'Brien's Shamrock Stable won $1,408,259 on the year, all of which was earned by horses trained by Ralph Martinez. O'Brien's horses won 230 of 796 races, which placed him second on the official list of owners ranked by wins behind Michael Gill's 487 wins from 2885 starts. Third on the list of winning owners with 128 wins from 1055 starts was Dale Baird.

Working exclusively for O'Brien, Martinez' wins as a trainer duplicated O'Brien's wins as an owner. The 230 wins put Martinez in sixth place nationally among trainers ranked by wins, behind high-profile Steve Asmussen, Scott Lake, Jerry Hollendorfer, Cole Norman, and Todd Pletcher—the same position Martinez had finished the previous year. Martinez' winning ratio of twenty-nine percent was the highest in the country; he was leading trainer at Hoosier Park for the second consecutive year with 62 wins from 197 starters; and he did particularly well at Fairmount Park, his home track, successfully defending his trainer championship with 143 wins from 513 starters during the 102-day meet.

"I want to win," Martinez said in a *Blood-Horse* interview with James Platz, "and I'm not going to lie and say I don't. Everybody asks if I want to be the leading trainer; well, of course I do. With being a leading trainer, you win a lot of races and make a lot of money. It all comes full circle. At the same time, it's a lot of work knowing where all the horses are, shipping horses around, and getting it all done. It takes a lot of people—it's not just me."

Jockey Ramsey Zimmerman finished in 4th place nationally with 326 wins, most through his first call connection with Martinez and O'Brien.

It had been, in many ways, a routine year for the Dale Baird Stable as the trainer ground out 131 wins and $2,063,884 in money won, again placing him number one at Mountaineer in wins and purse money. Nationally he ranked twentieth in wins as a trainer, and third as an owner with 128 wins. For most trainers, those numbers would represent the apex of a career; for Baird it was business as usual. In fact, his twelve-percent win percentage was mildly disappointing. But for other reasons, 2004 would be a year Baird would remember.

On the fifth of November, at Mountaineer Race Track, Baird's Frazee's Folly won the 8th race, a $7,500 claiming race. The only notable aspect of the race was that it was Baird's 9,000th lifetime win, a record-setting milestone not likely to be matched; Baird's good friend, Jack Van Berg, is in second place, more than 2,500 wins behind. "I have no plans to retire," said Baird. "If I can keep going long enough I'll hopefully get to 10,000 before the turn of another century."

At the end of the year Baird was notified that he would be receiving a special Eclipse Award in recognition of his training accomplishments. Despite the fact that he had led the trainer's annual list of winners 15 times and led the owner's list 17 times, this would be his first Eclipse Award. The recognition may have been overdue, but Baird was typically modest and appreciative. "It's quite an honor," he said with customary understatement.

6

Pssst... Are You Sure *You Don't Wanna Buy a Horse?*

From the middle of December through Christmas the Chicago area had been cold enough that the several inches of snow that fell a week before the holidays were preserved by the sub-zero temperatures. It was a white Christmas, and it would be another frosty-but-clear day for attendees to cope with at Dan Arrigo's annual Horses of Racing Age Sale at Hawthorne Race Course on December 28.

Forty-nine horses were cataloged, and Arrigo set a $500 minimum bid level, again to discourage horse killers from buying for slaughter. "They're all pickles," said Arrigo, "but most are sound and could be useful if shipped to a track with lesser competition." With typical puckish humor Arrigo prominently placed a near uncollectible inducement in the catalog: "*NOTICE!* Anyone who is in the money in a graded stake in 2005 with a horse out of this sale will get a bonus of *3 times* the fall of the hammer price."—an occurrence as likely to happen as back-to-back-to-back Triple Crown winners.

The paddock sale had again attracted two giants of the claiming game. The tallish Dale Baird, easily recognizable, wearing his perpetual grin, signature blue baseball cap and windbreaker, had driven in from West Virginia and was graciously accepting congratulations on his recent accomplishments while exchanging war stories with long-time acquaintances. Ralph Martinez, also wearing a baseball cap with a stylishly rolled bill pulled low over his eyes, his customary down jacket and blue jeans, was on the opposite side of the auction ring quietly studying the catalog for horses that could win a race or two at Fairmount Park. Few of those present recognized Martinez as the top percentage-winning trainer in the country.

The crowd consisted of the usual suspects: a few trainers from Great Lakes Downs, Fairmount Park and other small tracks, a handful of prospective owners, several Hawthorne trainers chatting up potential new owners, and a small group of excitable young women interested in buying a riding horse or two if the price was right. The crowd was cliquish and subdued, with most of the noise coming from the warmth-generating stomping of feet and blowing on hands; it was a group anxious to be done with the business at hand so they could move on to other, more comfortable matters.

John Anthony was the first horse to go through the ring. Having recently run in $5,000 claiming races for non-winners of 2 lifetime, the four-year-old bay gelding brought $650. The second horse through the ring, Proud and Steady, sold for the minimum and will likely wind up as a riding horse, having lost his last three races by a combined 55 lengths.

Next up was the regally named, obscurely bred Sir Allen, by Allen Charge out of A Queen's World, by Transworld. In 17 maiden claiming starts at Great Lakes Downs and Hawthorne, the three-year-old dark brown or bay gelding had yet to find the winner's circle, but Ralph Martinez saw something not evident to lesser sensitivities. Martinez' bid of $900 bought him a Fairmount Park reclamation project. "Well," the trainer said later, "it looks like the horse has a little speed, plus he was bred in Illinois which makes him eligible for state-bred awards. If we can win one race with him we're out on him. He's been in the money nine of seventeen times and earned more than $11,000, so the $900 doesn't seem like a big risk."

Martinez was also the high bidder on two of the final three horses in the sale, both of which were Illinois-breds, qualifying them for lucrative state-bred races and bonuses. Riverdance Tour, a five-year-old Tour d'Or gelding with four wins from 52 starts and lifetime earnings exceeding $100,000, was bought for $3,200. During the year the horse had raced at Arlington Park, Hawthorne and Mountaineer in sprints and middle-distance races at the $4–$10,000 claiming level. "He's a handy type of horse to have. He's a runner, and being an Illinois-bred will help him earn out real quick."

Lusty Kelly, a three-year-old filly eligible for non-winners of three races, was the last horse in the sale. By sprint sire Kipper Kelly, Lusty Kelly fit a recognizable Martinez profile: she was foaled in Illinois, showed early speed in her races, had some good conditions left, and though six furlongs seemed beyond her best distance she would be a good fit for the short four- and five-furlong races at Turfway Park and Fairmount. She had some back class, having run in a state-bred stakes as a two-year-old, but had recently been running for a $5,000 tag.

Dale Baird had been to too many auctions and bid on too many horses to get "auction fever," the urge to bid beyond what reason and circumstances dictated. The numerous Illinois-bred horses available (and the state-bred awards program) meant nothing to Baird because he races almost exclusively at West Virginia and Ohio tracks. He bid on a handful of horses but maintained a firm ceiling on his bidding. Baird had evaluated the horses prior to the sale and guesstimated what they might be worth to him running at Mountaineer

Park. He established maximum bids and stuck to them. As a result he wound up with just one horse, a five-year-old veteran by Marked Tree out of Gray Mackinaw, by Silver Buck, which had won four of thirty-five lifetime starts. In 2004 the horse had competed both in claiming and starter allowance races at Chicago tracks and had earned $27,115. Showing stalking speed going middle distances, the horse's style and abilities would seem to be a good fit for the tight turns at Mountaineer Park.

At the end of the sale twenty-five horses had been sold for $46,050, an average of $1,842 and a median of $900.

Four days after Arrigo's paddock sale Baird returned to Hawthorne and privately purchased six additional horses.

7

How You Gonna Keep 'Em Down on the Farm...?

Many Thoroughbreds are retired each year from the rigors of racing for varying reasons. Call Me Loverboy was physically spent. To continue his racing career would have put his welfare in jeopardy. Other horses, such as the high-profile 2006 Kentucky Derby winner Barbaro and runner-up Bluegrass Cat, sustained injuries necessitating immediate retirement. Others fared worse, such as Dr. Robbie. The 2005 Kentucky Derby winner, Giacomo, was retired in 2006 for breeding purposes. But not all of the retirees are ready to lead either a hedonistic or pastoral life....

As his groom led the visibly tired alabaster-hewn god-horse off the Arlington Park racetrack, his trainer knew it was over, that after a career spanning ten years and 81 races at the upper levels of the sport, it was time to retire the legendary gray-white runner named after the Navajo word for ghost.

Chindi, one of the Midwest's most popular and stylishly compelling Thoroughbred sprinters of all time due to his dramatic off-the-pace stretch-running style and distinctive pale coat accentuated by his regally long flowing tail, walked away from the track sound; it was not as if he had been a golden-aged Spartacus whipping up on lions from a walker or Superman fighting off kryptonite from a wheelchair ... it was more a case of long-haired biblical strongman Samson having to cope with a strength-sapping crew cut. Even though Chindi physically had come out of his races as an 11-year-old about the same as he had as a 3-year-old, his trainer Steve Hobby, an ex-jockey who has been training since 1976, felt the multiple stakes winner had lost his aggressive mental edge. "It was time," said Hobby. "His first two races of the year at Oaklawn Park were good efforts. He won a six-furlong optional claimer in February coming from dead last, 9 lengths off the lead, and then finished third by a closing half length in a similarly run race in April. The third-place purse money put him over $1,000,000 in money won, but regardless of his earnings I always told his owner, Carol Ricks (CresRan Stable), that I'd let her know when it was time to retire him."

Mrs. Ricks' late husband, Ran, bought Chindi in 1995 as a weanling from a breeder friend who had recently acquired Chindi's dam, Rousing, in foal to El Prado (Ire.), from the late Kentucky breeder Lockhart Spears of Stoneleigh Farm, and Heywood Hale Broun, the latter a popular stage and screen character actor and sporting journalist of note. Rousing's new owner was not interested in racing her offspring, consequently selling the El Prado-Rousing weanling to Ran Ricks, who died a few months after acquiring the weanling that became Chindi for CresRan Stable, adding poignancy to the legend of Chindi. Mrs. Ricks was determined that Chindi would always be well cared for both during and following his racing career.

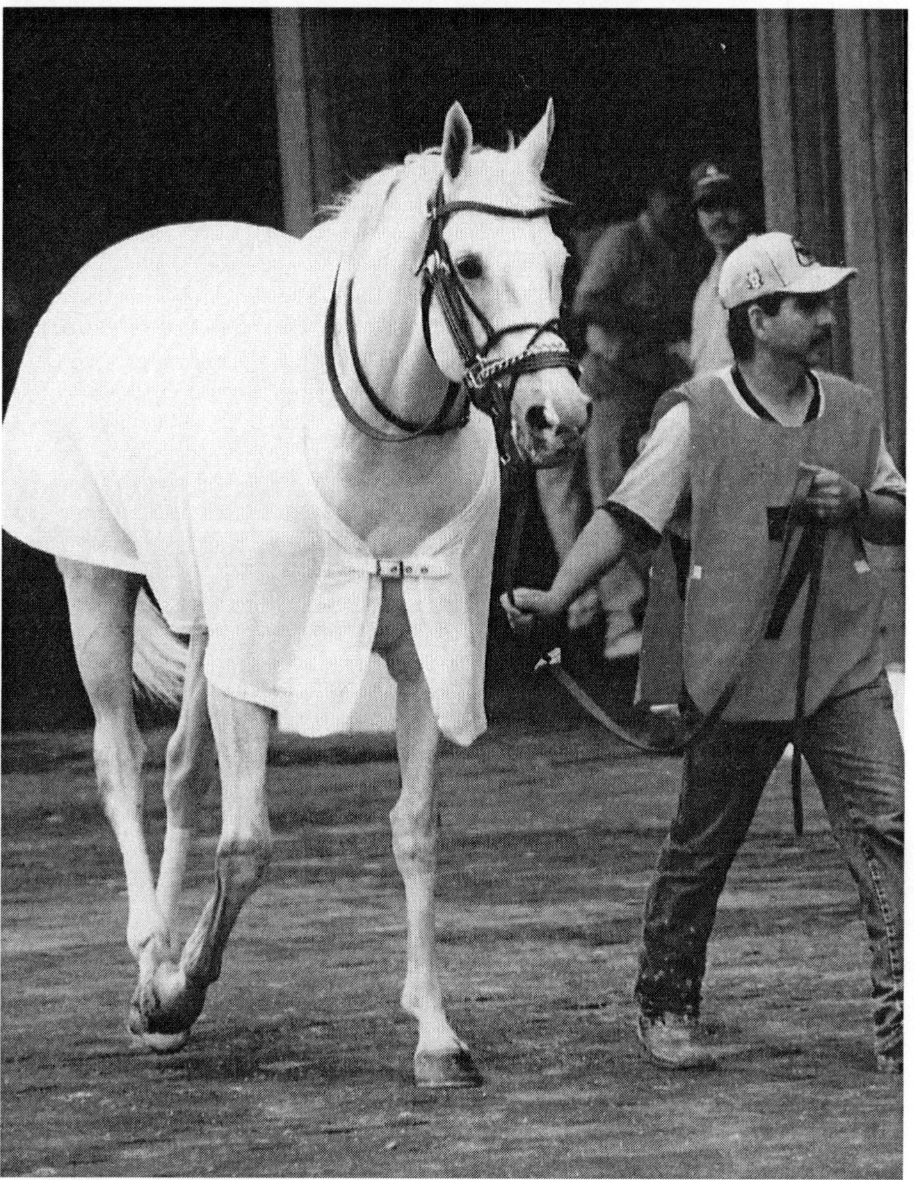

Being led to his stall in the Arlington Park paddock prior to his 81st and final race, Chindi retired 100 percent sound.

Chindi's third out of 2005 came on July 3rd in the six-furlong Better Bee Stakes at Arlington and proved less than satisfactory to Hobby. "He had always been a very confident horse, but he just seemed to go through the motions, finishing unplaced, not showing his usual finishing kick. He hadn't trained well for the race and while he was never a good work horse he acted as though he had lost a little of his competitive nature. We could have run him in small stakes at lesser tracks but didn't want to take a chance on getting him hurt, so we retired him after the Better Bee. We didn't make it official until the following spring when Oaklawn was able to have a special Chindi retirement appreciation day ceremony early in April [2006]. He had won a lot of races at Oaklawn and had many fans there who wished him well."

Shown racing in the CresRan Stable's light blue with brown band silks for the final time, Chindi retired with 18 wins and earnings of more than $1,000,000. Calvin Borel is the jockey.

Life at the track didn't end for Chindi when his racing days were over, however. "Several times over the years we had turned Chindi out on the Ricks farm for routine rest and rehabbing," said Hobby, "but he always seemed to be bored on the farm. He would walk the fences, pacing up and down, and then return to his stall as soon as possible. Each time we brought him back to the track he would come to life and be his typically aggressive self. Because he was a gelding he had no chance at a breeding career, so it was decided well before we actually retired him that he would be my stable pony instead of just putting him out to pasture. Working him as a stable pony we could keep him at the track around other horses where he would be involved in the daily activities of a racetrack."

It can be challenging to convert a high-strung racehorse into a

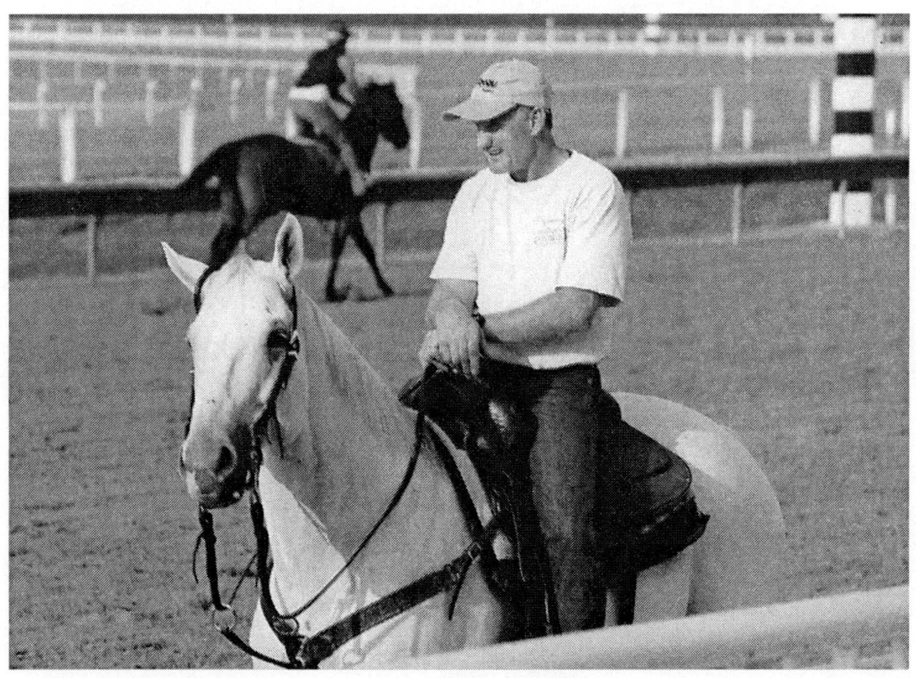

Chindi's workday now consists of giving trainer Steve Hobby a ride to and from the track during morning training hours.

command-driven stable pony, but for the track-wise Chindi, whom Hobby calls the smartest horse he has ever been around, the conversion was natural.

"Never really had to re-train him at all," said Hobby. "One day he was a racehorse, the next day he was a stable pony with me on his back leading a string of horses for early morning training. About the only thing different was the Western saddle on his back. He'd been around the track for so long he easily picked up on everything new we asked him to do. You could say it either took us one day to convert him to a stable pony or eleven years, depending on your point of view. His duties around the stable are pretty simple. His workday consists of giving me a ride to and from the track during training hours. When training is finished about nine or so we return to the stable where he rolls in a sand pit behind the stable and is then given a good bath. After his bath he is turned out in a paddock we have in front of the stables to eat grass and just be a horse. When he's had enough of grazing he lets us know and he's put back in his stall where he always manages to wrangle a few treats: carrots, mints, apples, bananas, just about anything. Keeping him active at the track was the right thing to do. He is a totally happy horse, and he is also the stable, or herd, boss. If a horse starts to get ornery or out of line Chindi will communicate his displeasure to the offending horse."

As he raced through his equine senior years it was no surprise that Chindi's best interests were foremost in the intentions of both his owner and trainer as he had always been a well-managed racehorse. "He never required anything special by way of training," said Hobby. "In the stable he has always had a good healthy appetite with no quirks but in the mornings on the training track he was a bad work horse. Because he hadn't shown much I entered him in a $25,000 maiden claimer at Oaklawn the first time we ran him. We may not have known what we had on our hands before the race but we found out quickly. Chindi won the six-furlong race by eight easy lengths pulling away in the stretch. That's the first and only time we ran him for a price."

Chindi's stylish pedigree, being sired by prominent turf and dirt stallion El Prado (Ire.) out of the aforementioned Rousing by classic runner Alydar, indicated that middle and classic distance races, most likely on the grass, would suit him best. El Prado was bred and raced in Ireland, where he won three stakes as a precocious 2-year-old, performances that won him the 2-year-old Irish championship, although none of his races were beyond a mile despite El Prado's having been sired by Sadler's Wells, one of the top classic distance-producing sires of all time. Sadler's Wells was in turn sired by Northern Dancer, winner of the Kentucky Derby and Preakness stakes, both races of which are considered by U.S. breeders to be of classic stature. El Prado's dam, Lady Capulet, was sired by English Derby winner Sir Ivor. Alydar, Chindi's broodmare sire, is best remembered for having finished close seconds to Affirmed in all three 1978 Triple Crown races.

After just a handful of races, two of which found Chindi experimentally going a mile over the grass, Hobby knew that pedigree could be set aside: Chindi was a late-closing sprinter possessing a dynamite blast of a quarter-mile spurt who did not like to run long and did not like to run over the turf. And he especially did not like to be rushed from the gate. "Actually he breaks good from the gate," explained Hobby. "He gets a good first jump from the gate but after the first stride or so he slows himself down. No real reason for it; it's just his style. And while he is a nicely balanced horse, about 15.2 or 15.3 hands, he is short-legged and has a short stride, which requires extra effort on his part and explains why he was most effective running in sprints. The 7½-furlong distance of the Ack Ack stakes races he ran in at Churchill Downs were about as long as he could handle. His very best distance may have been 6½ furlongs, just long enough to let some of the sharp speed start to come back to him."

The ghost horse would go on to race 81 times, posting 18 wins, 13 seconds and 23 third-place finishes for earnings totaling $1,000,838. All but two of his races were at 7½ furlongs or less;

fifty-four were at the sprint standard of six furlongs. He ran in ten graded stakes races, winning the 6-furlong Grade 3 Count Fleet Sprint Handicap at Oaklawn in 1999 by coming from eleven lengths off the pace, and the 7½-furlong Grade 3 Ack Ack Handicap at Churchill Downs in 2000, coming from 14 lengths off the pace around the final turn. His most awe-inspiring race may have been the 6-furlong $100,000 Taylor's Special Handicap, also in 2000. Chindi took advantage of the long stretch at the Fairgrounds in New Orleans to make up 15 lengths running six wide from the top of the stretch to the finish line to win on the wire by a neck. He never ran beyond a mile, and while it was readily apparent to Hobby that Chindi had distance limitations, he did not have to be coddled by running only at a particularly advantageous track or under ideal

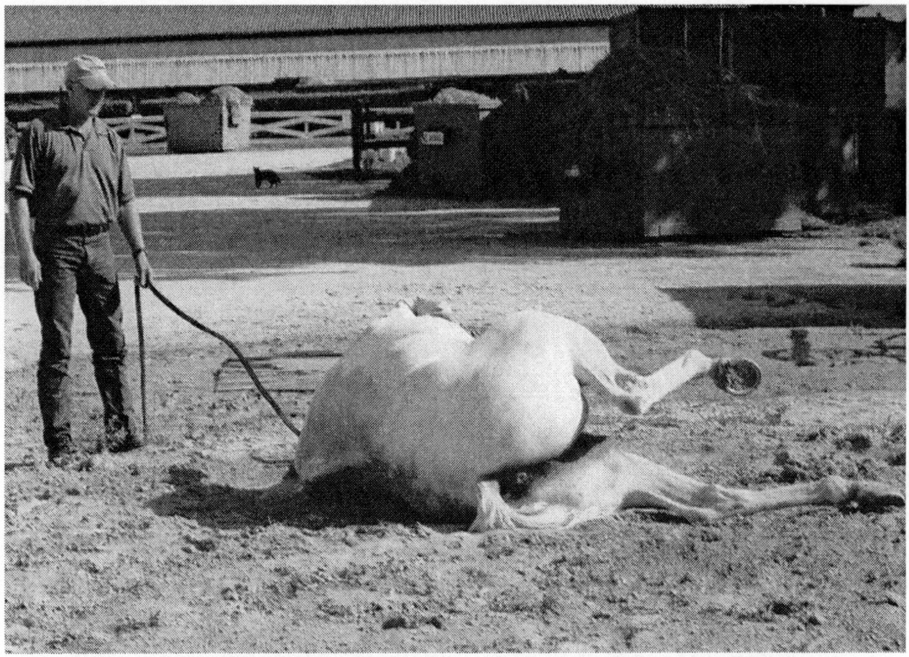

After completing his training duties, Chindi is taken to the sandpit outside of his stall where he gets down on his knees, flops over and rolls from side to side in the sand. Life is good.

Following his roll in the sand, Chindi is given a soothing bath, restoring the luster on his near-white coat.

conditions. He raced at a total of thirteen tracks and fast or wet conditions made no difference in his performance. Tim Doocy, a patient come-from-behind rider who Hobby felt understood Chindi's need to make one very late run, was Chindi's regular jockey throughout the majority of his career, riding him in 45 races. Further testimony to Hobby's sensible track management of his stable star is the fact that Chindi was 10–1 or more on the odds board just nine times and was never more than 18–1, meaning that the horse was entered where he had a common-sense chance to be competitive. Three of his long-shot races occurred near the end of his career when hard-core bettors erroneously doubted the ability of the old sprinter to run at a continuing high level of competition.

I. At the Track

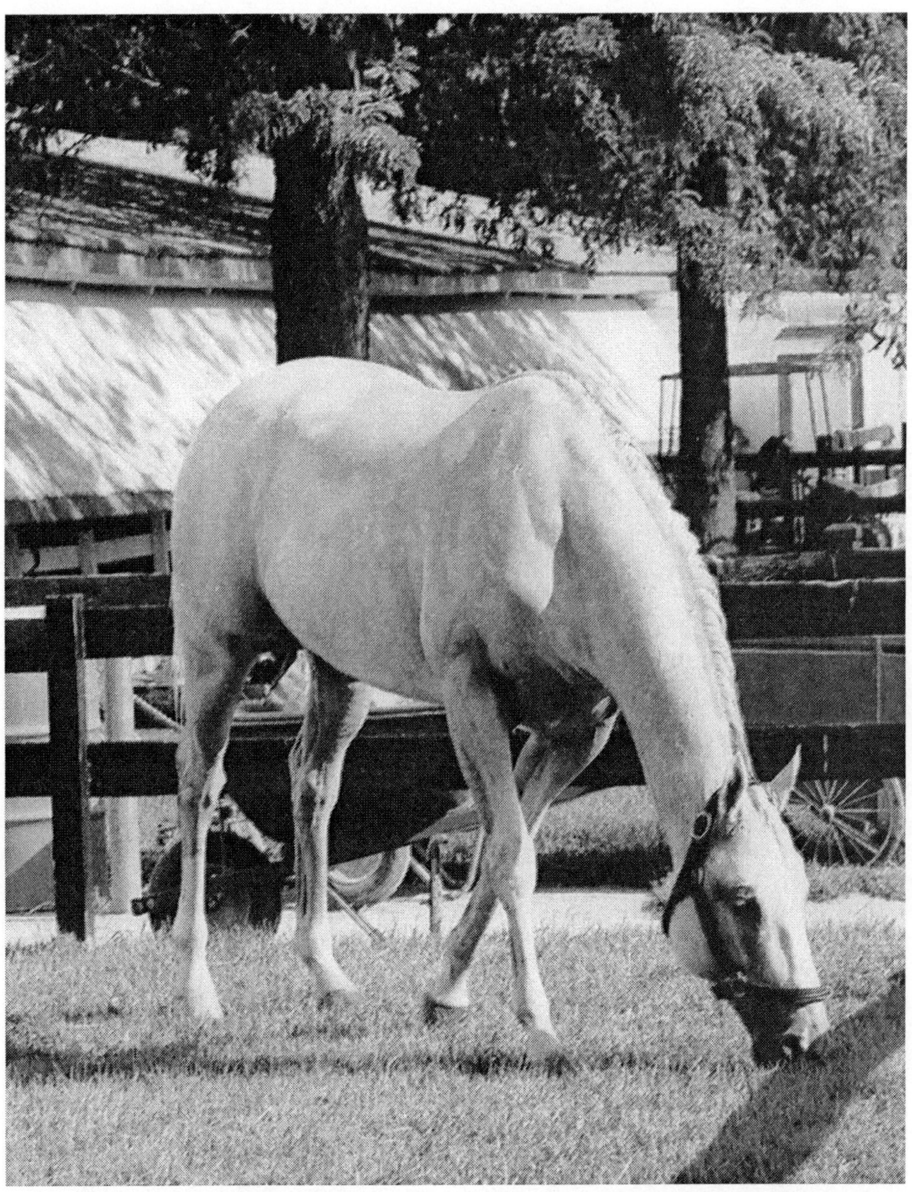

Before returning to his stall for snacks, the equine stable boss is allowed to graze as long as he chooses.

7. How You Gonna Keep 'Em Down on the Farm...?

Chindi was born well into a good family and raised right. He was successful at his day job and now enjoys a well-earned semi-retirement surrounded by those whose lives he touched. The saga of Chindi is an adventurous Navajo ghost story with a happy ending.

II

On the Farm

Dream big, and why not? Morgan McDonnell is shown with gray mare Appalachee Wolf, her foal and potential Derby/Oaks winner Captain Fluffy, and youngest daughter Kit. The McDonnells live in the former home of Marguerite Henry, renowned author of *Misty of Chincoteague* and numerous other equine books for children.

II. On the Farm

Every proud parent's new baby boy will be the next president; each new baby girl will be a movie star ... or the next president. For horse breeders each new foal will be a stout-legged missile destined for Kentucky Derby greatness and beyond.

Logic and rational thinking aside, there's no reason why a one-mare breeder can't have the same dreams as the luxurious, sprawling mega-sized breeding farms. There is precedent for such fantasies becoming reality and the odds are much better than winning the lottery.

8

Mole Meadows and the House of Optimism

Dream no small dreams for they have no power to move the hearts of men.

—*Johann Wolfgang von Goethe.*

My goal, at least the one I tell my family and friends, is to win the [Kentucky] Derby and the [English] Darby. In this business you have to dream big; you have to enjoy the dream because the highs are so few. Besides, winning the Derby is more likely than winning the lottery.

—*Morgan McDonnell, Mole Meadows.*

She was certainly no racehorse—couldn't get six furlongs in anything less than two minutes—but Misty, the equine heroine of many Marguerite Henry children's books, was a for-real, flesh and blood, silver-and-gold-hued pony that could be touched and ridden, unlike fictional horses such as Black Beauty, Flicka, and other four-legged favorites whose actions were dictated entirely by the imaginations of their respective literary creators.

The exploits of the white-blazed endearing hero of *Misty of Chincoteague* were documented and romanticized by the late children's author Marguerite Henry (1902–1997), throughout the 1940s and '50s. Henry's stories of the trials and tribulations of the little Spanish Moor pony have spawned a legacy carried on through the dreams of generations of young people, youthful equestrians-to-be who fantasized of owning a pony or showing a horse long before any thoughts of prom dates or S.A.T. scores entered their consciousness. If the real Misty has long since gone off to horse heaven (in storybook fashion, she died in her sleep in 1972 at 26), the pony's literary reputation remains solidly in place through numerous reprints of Henry's stories.

The legend put to paper half a century ago continues to this day at Misty's former Wayne, Illinois, residence known to her knowledgeable readers as "Mole Meadows," a two-acre bucolic horse farm *cum* residential estate cloistered among mature landscaping set back from the hustle of a former Indian trail turned roadway, obscured by trees and spreading shrubs that were part of the landscape when Misty was just a foal. The comfortable yellow wood frame cottage where Marguerite and her husband Sid Henry lived—and where Misty was a long-time beloved resident—now serves as home to the McDonnell family: Morgan, his wife Kappo, and their two children, Martha and Kit. Misty's barn has been converted to a functioning business office for McDonnell's import/export business, but from outward appearances it has not changed at all from the time it served as Misty's stable. Now, however, nearby pasture land is home to several young Kentucky Derby and English "Darby" hopefuls whose story, should their owner's dreams be fulfilled, would be every bit as inspiring—although far more improbable than any Black Beauty fiction—as Marguerite Henry's tall but true tales.

8. Mole Meadows and the House of Optimism

Wayne is a sparsely populated, affluent clone of a New England village situated thirty-five miles west of Chicago smack in the middle of Midwest horse country. It is a blend of barns, horses, tree-lined streets without sidewalks, low speed limits and high property taxes. There are a total of three retail businesses in the village: a country store (vintage enough in appearance to have been used as a location site for several movies requiring an authentic country store setting), a one-pump gas station-turned-car-repair, and an art gallery that specializes in horse and dog paintings. Too small in populace to appear on most maps, Wayne has achieved more than a certain renown as the creative birthplace of the Misty stories: more than a century ago, long before Marguerite Henry's animal and pony stories, the village could boast of a different sort of international fame throughout the equine world.

The area's preeminence in nineteenth-century equine activities can be directly attributed to Solomon Dunham, an entrepreneurial farmer who, in 1836, moved his family from Erie County, New York, to the sparsely wooded farmland now known as Wayne. In short order Dunham's aggressiveness and business acumen put him in the forefront of the village's founding movers and shakers. He purchased a 300-acre tract that he named Oaklawn Farm, and which subsequently grew to 1,700 acres as it established a glossy reputation as one of the largest and best equipped livestock breeding farms in the country. Dunham also served as one of the county's commissioners; he was the first county assessor, the first station agent and Wayne's first postmaster. In his spare time he worked as a surveyor for the now-defunct Galena & Chicago Union Railroad, and it was his efforts in that capacity that caused the railroad to route its tracks through western DuPage County, where Dunham owned extensive acreage.

Solomon Dunham's interest in livestock breeding was inherited by his son Mark (1842–1899), who was a chip off the entrepreneurial block, although young Dunham preferred to focus his energies on the importation and consequent breeding of Percherons, large draft horses used for farm work, hauling circus wagons (in addition to actually performing in various circus acts) and for any other utility work requiring the power and pulling strength of brawny livestock. Years later Marguerite Henry would say, "It's exciting to me that no matter how much machinery replaces the horse, the work it can do is still measured in horsepower.... And although a riding horse often weighs a half a ton and a big drafter a full ton, either can be led about by a piece of string if he has been wisely trained." For decades Mark Dunham made annual trips to Europe, particularly France, Belgium and England, to purchase Percherons for Oaklawn Farm. It was not unusual for Dunham to acquire a hundred or more head a year at a cost that could reach the then-extravagant sum of $5,000 for a particularly notable specimen ... enough money to buy ten Model T Fords, had they yet been invented.

When the Percheron Horse Association of America was formed in 1876, Dunham was one of its fourteen founding directors, and he remained active in association activities until his death in 1899. As further documentation of Dunham's horse fervor, he is credited with importing more than 300 stallions and 75 mares between 1872 and 1880, capped by the importation of the breed's primary foundation sire, Brilliant 1271, which stood at stud at Oaklawn Farm for 15 years. The horse's description in a contemporary Oaklawn Farm catalog defines the ideal Percheron: *"Weight: 1,850; 16 hands high. Long and very round body; extraordinary length of quarters, which are broad and level; very sloping shoulders of unusual depth; neck rather short; medium throttle; fine ear; wide between the eyes; slightly Roman nose; very broad breast; short legs and bone of uncommon width; immense stifle power. A horse with a combination of excellencies throughout."*

Oaklawn Farm, whose advertisements in the trade papers claimed it to be "the largest importing and breeding establishment in the world," reached the zenith of its celebrity in 1892, when it was listed as one of the points of interest for the World's Columbian Exposition (Fair) held in Chicago. In conjunction with the World's Fair, the United States Government selected Dunham's showplace as one of just two farms to be visited by the Pan-American Congress—a group of influential politicos representing seventeen independent nations of North and South America—during their tour of the United States (the other farm was Henry Clay's historic Ashland estate in Kentucky). A direct descendent of Christopher Columbus, the Duke of Veragua, was a member of the celebrated entourage assembled to discover advances in American agriculture.

Today the Dunham Woods Riding Club, located on a portion of now subdivided Oaklawn Farm, is the hub of Wayne's horsey tradition. Directly west of the club are two further reminders of the Dunham family and Wayne's salad days as the epicenter of Percheron breeding: Dunham Road is a major north-south roadway connecting several major northeast Illinois cities, and about a furlong from the country club stands the iconic, imperial Dunham Castle, a French chateau-inspired castle replete with turrets, battlements, all the accouterments a castle might need to repel the unwanted masses except a moat. The Dunham Castle has fought off encroaching urban development and even a period during which its interior was subdivided into apartments. It has since been restored to its initial splendor and now serves as a private residence.

The Wayne horse culture is further nurtured by the fact that it is within short cantering distance of five hunt clubs, three racetracks and numerous breeding farms and training facilities. Miles of horse trails wind through the sections of western DuPage and eastern Kane Counties where Wayne is situated and where Misty of Chincoteague, Blighty the Burro, The King of the Wind Arabian and other Henry heroes became an indelible childhood recollection in the fond memories of near-countless junior riders.

Since 1989 Morgan McDonnell has been the master of Mole Meadows. No stranger to either the business or sporting side of horses, McDonnell has been active in international trade markets as an importer/exporter of horses and complementary products for most of his adult life, traveling in the heady, sophisticated company of the equine gentrified set, sportsmen who support the breed on various world-class levels: riding to hounds, jumping, showing, racing and polo. As a jet-setting global businessman and gentleman horse trader, McDonnell has been to more race tracks in more countries than there are Arabian nights, with many of the exotic sites rivaling the mystique of the barrier islands in the Atlantic Ocean off the coasts of Maryland and Virginia which were the physical birthplace of Misty as well as herds of then-nondescript Moorish ponies.

Having been raised both on the legend of ponderous Percherons and the local pony heroine Misty, exposed to all equine disciplines at an early age through active competition, McDonnell not only learned to dream big derby dreams in Technicolor, he also

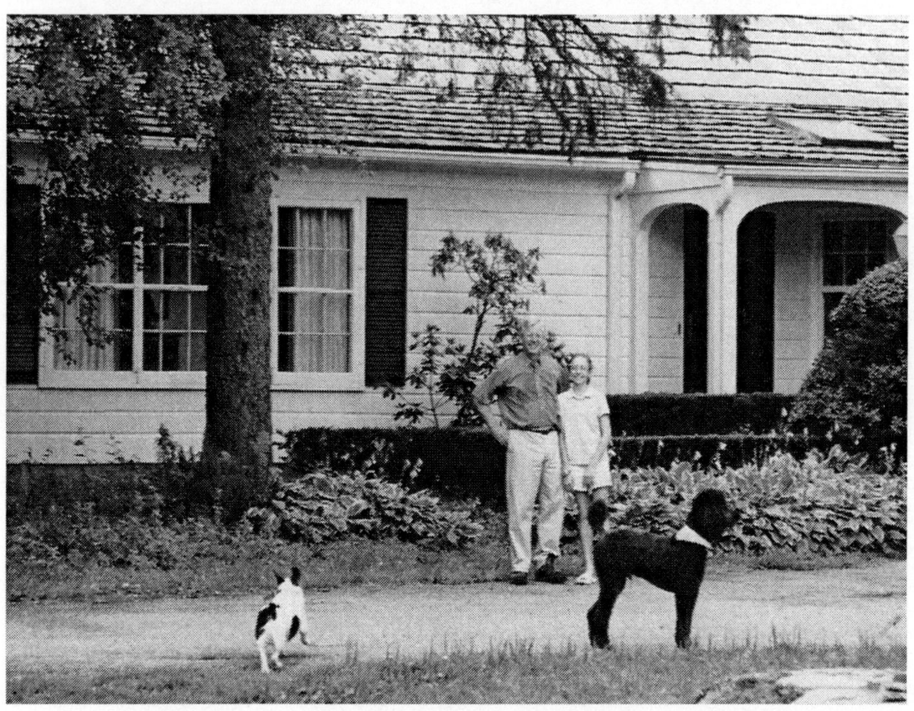

Morgan McDonnell and his daughter Kit, with two family members, outside their historic home, Mole Meadows, in Wayne, Illinois.

developed the knack of pragmatically converting the wispy vapors of dreamland into reality. Growing up in the midst of an active horse community, it was a boyhood dream of McDonnell's to become more than an obligatory participant in local hunting, jumping and dressage events at the family club. He wanted to be at the white-hot center of equine sport, to become a jockey, to be able to feel the thrust and power of a Thoroughbred in its ultimate competition: racing flat out, surging to the head of the herd. In 1985, at thirty-three, an age when jockeys are considered to be middle-aged and set in their career path, McDonnell became one of the oldest "apprentice" jockeys in history when he was given a leg up on a mount during the race meet at Phoenix Park just inside the city limits of Dublin, Ireland, 3,000 miles from his Mole Meadows stables. To McDonnell the trip seemed much longer than the seven-hour plane trip, and every bit as improbable as his later dream of breeding and racing classic derby winners.

McDonnell's lifelong obsession to ride competitively in Thoroughbred races had begun to grow more remote as his personal life and business career matured despite the fact that he had been an active participant in many equine sporting activities well into his thirties, and had ridden in a number of steeplechase races, a dangerous second cousin to Thoroughbred flat racing. A steeplechase race is slower to develop than a Thoroughbred race but relies heavily on the mental and physical dexterity of both horse and rider as they calculate the successful jumping of a series of fences, or hurdles, on the way from the starting tape to the finish line, creating sporting obstacles that require teamwork and coordination. It is a risky sport for participants, but for McDonnell it lacked the flat-out speed and flair of Thoroughbred racing. Ironically, it was a champion Irish steeplechase rider who was responsible for McDonnell's debut as a Thoroughbred jockey.

"I was, and am, in the business of buying and selling horses, Thoroughbreds as well as other breeds, for hunting, jumping, racing ... for most equine disciplines," McDonnell explained. "My customers and associates are spread worldwide. During the '80s I was doing a lot of business through the late John Harty, a champion Irish steeplechase jockey who, like myself, had become somewhat of a bloodstock agent. We were partners on many deals and our business relationship grew into a strong friendship.

"During the first week of August in 1985 I was in Ireland to attend the Dublin Horse Show with Harty, participating both as a buyer and seller. The Dublin show is a massive event at which a thousand or more horses of all types, shapes and sizes are offered for sale in an informal, country fair atmosphere. As a complement to the show, the now-defunct Phoenix Park annually held a short race meet that Harty and I usually attended. This particular year one of the jockeys happened to get injured shortly before the start of a two-mile 'Mad Hatter' amateur rider's race on the flat. 'Now's your chance to be a jock,' said Harty, as he quickly volunteered my services to the racing officials with tongue-in-cheek, eyes averted, and fingers crossed. The licensing obligations were a bit more lax back then, at least at Phoenix Park, and before I had much of a chance to savor the opportunity, or, more wisely, reconsider, I was galloping bug-eyed around the track in my first race on the flat along with 24 other horses being guided by amateur riders. The ride was exhausting; my legs were like mush when I dismounted, but I was, finally, officially a flat-race jockey with a third-place finish to my credit. I rode again the next year at the same meet, one final time, and though I continued to ride as an amateur in many steeplechase races in the States during the next ten years I never again rode on the flat."

McDonnell had been a horseman-in-waiting since childhood when he attended the local riding school and pestered Eddie Pacuinas, the trainer of Misty, Jose the Donkey and other Henry characters, for lessons. He worked his way through amateur hunt and jumping competitions, always with the ultimate goal of becoming a jockey. "When I was a teenager I tried to get a job exercising horses for Richard Hazelton, who was a training legend even back then," McDonnell recalls. "I was introduced to Hazelton at Hawthorne

Race Course and worked some horses for him. Everything went smoothly and he told me to come back the next day to begin work. When I showed up at the barn the next day Hazelton had a sheepish, apologetic smile on his face. 'Kid,' he said, 'you did fine yesterday but I got to fire you before you start.' He nodded toward a smaller than average jockey a few feet away. 'Bill is rehabbing from a recent injury and needs to work horses in the mornings to get back into shape so I gotta give him the job. You can tell people from now on that you lost your first racetrack job to Bill Shoemaker.' I've gotten more mileage telling the story than I ever would have had working horses for Hazelton, so everything worked out okay." Hazelton went on to win thousands of races, becoming the fourth most winning trainer in history, all of the wins being achieved without the assistance of Morgan McDonnell. Bill Shoemaker recovered to become the sport's all-time leading race-winning jockey at the time of his retirement.

For McDonnell, the personal evolution in the sport culminated around 1996 with the purchase, in partnership, of a Thoroughbred race mare. "When Kappo and I started a family, first with our daughter Martha and then with our second daughter Kit, it seemed prudent to forego competitive riding. The resultant void left me looking for a less hazardous activity but something that would still involve Thoroughbreds and racing. That's when a few friends and I bought Shirley Dear, a Thoroughbred mare with some races still left in her. She won several races and we had a lot of fun with her," he recalled, "but when Shirley's racing days were over the partnership voted to sell her. A few years later I bought Appalachee Wolf ('Wolfie'), a gray Wolf Power former race mare that I intended to use as a hunter. Unfortunately she developed a cataract about three years ago so I retired her from hunting and made a broodmare out of her. From her first breeding we have a 2004 yearling filly by Unreal Zeal named Are You Dancing. The following year we bred Wolfie to Chicago Six and got a 2005 filly my daughters call Captain Fluffy. In 2005 we bred her to Bold Revenue, a Bold Ruckus stallion that stands at Tower Farm in Somonauk, about an hour from here."

Having long been involved the financial give-and-take of the bloodstock business it was natural for McDonnell to assume a businesslike, analytical approach to the breeding of Appalachee Wolf. Scouring Brisnet.com, a Lexington, Kentucky-based online bloodstock research service, and then poring over various breeding manuals, he came to the conclusion that Wolf Power mares were especially productive when bred to the Mr. Prospector line, or nick. McDonnell inspected Mr. Prospector-line stallions under consideration and concluded that for her first mating Wolfie was to be sent a few miles north of Mole Meadows to be bred to the tempestuous but successful son of Mr. Prospector, Unreal Zeal, who was then standing at Horizon Farm in Barrington, Illinois. The stallion was known for a fiery temperament, a nasty trait tolerated because Zeal had established a reputation for siring precocious early runners that generated a quick payback for their owners. The resultant bay-but-turning-roan foal of Unreal Zeal-Appalachee Wolf, Are You Dancing, was healthy although "a little toed out early on, but as her body filled out her legs have straightened out nicely. Coat color aside, she looks a lot like Mr. Prospector," said McDonnell, well aware that Mr. Prospector progeny can have soundness issues. McDonnell is equally aware that Mr. P has sired some of the quickest and most valuable Thoroughbreds in the history of racing. The hope is that the good genetics would be passed on to Are You Dancing by his son, Unreal Zeal.

Two-time Illinois champion Chicago Six, Wolfie's second mate, is a young Wild Again stallion and a graded stakes winner of more than $700,000 standing at Richard Duchossois's Hill 'n Dale Farm in Barrington, Illinois, just minutes from Wayne. Wild Again was in turn sired by Icecapade, a half brother to Hall of Fame filly Ruffian, the ill-fated filly many consider the fastest female Thoroughbred of all time. Chicago Six doesn't include Mr. Prospector in his pedigree but has several crosses of Nearco, who figures prominently in Mr. P's pedigree. Chicago Six's broodmare sire is Triple Crown winner Secretariat, who has a much better reputation as a sire of broodmares than of stallions. To date, with her adolescent years and pitfalls still ahead of her, the foal is "Beautiful. Not a problem in the world with her," according to McDonnell.

For her third mating, McDonnell again kept Wolfie in Illinois ("I believe in dreaming big, but it doesn't hurt to hedge the genetic bet a little bit by breeding horses eligible for Illinois-bred breeder bonuses"), selecting Tower Farm's Bold Revenue, a stakes winner of 8 of 14 races while competing under the name Fozzi Bear. Sired by speedster Bold Ruckus, Bold Revenue has Bold Ruler and Nasrullah in the tail male line of his pedigree. Bold Revenue's female side also shows precocious speed through I'm For More, who was in turn sired by Olympia, a sprint specialist. Four generations back there are steadying influences on either side of Bold Revenue's pedigree, such as Preakness and Belmont winner Native Dancer, Double Jay, Heliopolis and Hill Prince. Bold Revenue is inbred 4x5 to Polynesian, who was a rowdy, willful horse most effective at shorter distances, but who sired dual classic winner Native Dancer.

An ancillary part of the joy of raising and racing Thoroughbreds for McDonnell is hands-on involvement. From initially selecting and purchasing Wolfie, to arranging the breedings and then breaking and giving the resultant foals their early, pre-track training, McDonnell is totally involved. Before the foals were able to stand and nurse he had selected his first choice as a trainer: long-time friend Billy Turner, the veteran trainer whose credentials include training Triple Crown winner Seattle Slew, would be given first opportunity to train McDonnell's derby hopefuls Are You Dancing and Captain Fluffy.

"The young Mole Meadows horses are handled a lot," said McDonnell. "I handle the weanling more than the yearling, but they are both easy to work with because of frequent exposure to humans and handling." The only aspect of raising his own Thoroughbreds that McDonnell entrusted to others was the actual foaling. "I wanted a pro to handle the foalings, especially when Wolfie was a maiden mare. We vanned her to nearby Tower Farm to take advantage of their state-of-the-art foaling and farm facilities. Everything went like clockwork and was totally without incident."

Tower Farm was not always the state-of-the-art thoroughbred breeding and boarding facility that it is now known to be. In fact, in the esoteric if not downright mystical witches'-brew realm of big-time horse breeding, Somonauk, Illinois, compares to Lexington, Kentucky, as the Soapbox Derby does to the Kentucky Derby.

Thoroughbred activity is scarce in Somonauk, a German-Irish-English ancestry farm community of 1,500; there is, in fact, no commercial Thoroughbred activity within a forty-mile radius, which is the way that Tower Farm's husband and wife owners (and only full-time employees) Wally and Janet Hartwig prefer it as they go about their considerable chores in a focused, unobstructed and realistic manner. Being the only fish in a small pond has not slowed the Hartwigs from developing their farm into an efficient model for contemporary equine husbandry.

Both of the Hartwigs have always had tunnel vision of what they wanted to accomplish in life, and how to go about it, starting from the day they met. "I was working in Chicago as an electrician at Western Electric," said Wally, "but had always had an interest in horses despite being a city boy. I had moved from inner-city Cicero to Lockport, where I had a small farm and some horses. Shortly after relocating to the Lockport farm I happened to attend the International Livestock Exposition where I saw Janet working the rodeo, riding barrel races. Soon as I saw her race by I knew she was the one for me." Despite promising Janet that he would give up the horse business if she married him (a campaign promise quickly and willingly ignored by both), things have worked out perfectly.

"When we bought the farm in 1971," said Wally, "it was just an 8-acre segment of what had been a much larger crop and sheep farm. It had become badly rundown and neglected. In what is now the primary stable we were literally up to our knees in sheep dung. During the thirty-five years Janet and I have owned the farm we have added an additional fifty acres, built three new barns, a breeding shed, three run-in sheds, a garage area, carved out three large pastures, three sand paddocks, two grass paddocks, a turn-out pen, and have enlarged the main house to three times the size it was when we first moved in. We don't have a set plan but every year we try to improve something, such as installing TV monitors and an intercom system in the foaling barn. Lately we have concentrated on improvements that will help lighten our load physically as well as improve things for the horses. We still grow a few crops—feed corn, soybeans—but it feels good to be able to say that the horses we breed, board or race have paid for it all." The Thoroughbred roster at any one time could include a mix of broodmares, foals, yearlings, and lay-ups, plus the two current stallions, Bold Revenue (Bold Ruckus-More Revenue by I'm For More) and Dandy's Secret (Riverman-Ack's Secret by Ack Ack). Previous stallions have included Mara Lark, Old Frankfort, Timely Counsel and Key Player.

The majority of the fifteen to twenty broodmares at Tower Farm are boarded for outside owners, and are shuttled to and from Kentucky to be bred. Additionally, the Hartwigs maintain several broodmares in order to breed one or two of their own foals each year. Lay-ups and other stock swell the Thoroughbred count to thirty-five or so head. While Wally philosophizes that "for every ten foals, maybe one or two really want to be racehorses," Tower Farm has had some success with Illinois-bred home-breds. Awholelotofmalarky, a hard-trying gelding known around both the racing stable and farm as Little John Henry, was one of their most notable runners.

A dark bay or brown foal of 1998, Malarky was sired by one of Tower Farm's own stallions, Dandy's Secret, and despite his relatively small stature the horse showed promise from the moment he set foot on the track. Unfortunately, it took several years to actually

When Wally Hartwig and his wife, Janet, bought a small portion of a crop and sheep farm in 1971 he was literally up to his knees in sheep dung. Now a successful Thoroughbred racing, breeding and boarding operation, the Hartwig's Tower Farm still keeps Wally up to his knees in farm by-products.

get him into the starting gate. "He wasn't a particularly large foal and we didn't feel he had matured enough to race at two," explained Janet Hartwig. "We turned him over to Hector Magana to race at three and it was Hector who started calling him Little John Henry. Malarky had a much better disposition than the real John Henry, but the two horses looked as though they could be identical twins: dark bay, unmarked, compact, standing only about 15.2 or 15.3 hands. And, like John Henry, Malarky always had suspicious knees. Magana got just one start out of him at three before we had to stop with him because of a knee problem.

"After laying Malarky up here at the farm for a number of months we brought him back as a four-year-old and despite a habit of pulling himself up near the finish line the little guy was able to break his maiden and more than pay his way. Malarky also had a bleeding problem that we were able to successfully treat, and adding a simple thing like a tongue-tie helped, too. Because he was not a particularly robust horse, and because he always tried so hard, we needed to give him at least three weeks between starts. He seemed to be able to run short or long, on dirt or grass, sloppy or fast track, whatever, as long as we gave him sufficient rest between starts. Unfortunately he developed chips in his right knee as a four-year-old, and then near the end of the year he cut his rear pastern running on snowy ground while turned out in his paddock here at the farm.

"When we brought Malarky back at five under new trainer Jerry Calvin he got left at the gate in his first start and then came on through the stretch as though he was Seabiscuit. We tried him at middle-distances on the grass for his next two races and he won them both, coming from off the pace. In the meantime, as a precautionary measure we had been having Malarky x-rayed regularly because of his previous knee problems. When we x-rayed after his second consecutive win we found out that he had damaged the same knee. The x-rays showed a stress fracture in his right knee. We could have gotten another start or two out of him but it might have proved fatal. We retired him; wound up giving him to Dot Morgan in Ohio, who finds homes for retired racehorses."

Awholelotofmalarky finished his career having won three races and nearly $100,000. It took him 19 starts to win the three races but at the very end of his injury-shortened career he showed that he possessed the combination of which every owner and breeder hopes for: heart, ability and desire. He wound up about $6,500,000 shy of what two-time Horse of the Year John Henry won during an 83-race career, but in addition to their physical similarities, Awholelotofmalarky shared another significant trait with John Henry, according to Wally Hartwig:

"Malarky was a real trier."

III

Riders Up

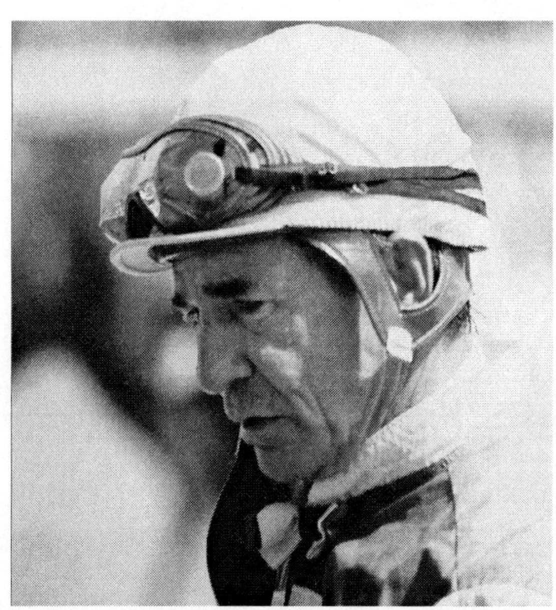

Earlie Fires was the leading apprentice jockey in the country in 1965. Now nearing sixty, the Hall of Fame jockey is still winning stakes races at major tracks, ranking tenth in all-time wins with more than 6,400 first-place finishes. Horses ridden by Fires have amassed approximately $85,000,000 in earnings.

III. Riders Up

Once the starting gate springs open and the horses bolt onto the racing surface, the race responsibility transfers into the vise-like grip of the jockey, a physically diminutive athlete who is charged with taming the wild herd mentality of an animal ten times his weight into an obedient racing machine. The breeder's work was finished years ago; the trainer's job ended when the horses first entered the track. It is the jockey who brings civilization to the race.

The rider uses minimal equipment to do his job: a saddle approximately half the size of a bikini bottom, a few strips of leather used to steer the horse, and a whip the size of a fly swatter. Thus equipped, the jock is charged with slowing his charge and then accelerating, all the while steering clear of other horses and riders who are also trying to get to the finish line first at maximum speed.

Race riding is an exhilarating, serious endeavor. During the running of a race a horse can take a bad step, suffer an injury or just stumble, sending its scantily protected rider into harm's way. Horses can suffer catastrophic injuries during a race; so can jockeys. Ron Turcotte, whom only a racing aficionado will remember as the regular rider of revered 1973 Triple Crown winner Secretariat, was paralyzed just a few years later in a racing accident.

He never walked again.

Yet it is the horse who is the hero in the mind of the average racing patron. It is the horse's past performances upon which odds are based, not the jockey's. And it is the horse on whom knowledgeable fans bet despite the fact that a top jockey like John Velazquez or Edgar Prado wins more stakes races in several months than even the top horses win in a lifetime of competition.

But it's never easy.

Breakfast of Champions

Gingerly swinging his scarred legs over the side of the bed, the veteran jockey repressed a persistent hacking smoker's cough while being careful not to wake his wife or to step on the pig sleeping on the floor; it was damn early and dark as always. Maneuvering about the ill-lit 40' travel trailer at five in the morning on legs made functional only by stainless steel surgical pins and knee-to-ankle screwed-in plates while at the same time trying not to disrupt his wife Cheri, son Kolten, or Silly Girl, their potbelly pig—who will all soon enough be up to go to work, school or simply root around—is a challenge, but not as difficult as what awaits him: Newil Wall is a 57-year-old jockey riding the bullring Nebraska circuit. The tracks open for training at 6 A.M. in the summer, 7 A.M. in the winter, and Wall likes to get started as soon as possible, especially during the summer months when the heat from the plains is hard on the horses, creating a higher incidence of bleeding, among other things.

III. Riders Up

"I don't eat no breakfast," says Wall, patting his plumb line-flat stomach, hobbling about the kitchen, looking for matches. "Never drank a cup of coffee in my life. For me, breakfast is a can of Coke. Got nothin' against Pepsi or other colas, but first thing in the morning I need a *Coke*. Need a cigarette, too. Then just before I leave for the track I'll put a pot of coffee on for Cheri so it's ready for her when she gets up. She works in the mutual department at Fonner so I'll usually see her later in the day. Kolten works as a runner in the jockey's room for tips after school, so we are really a racetrack family." Cupboard doors opening and shutting, cups being pulled for coffee don't seem to wake Wall's wife, son or pig.

"Once I'm up and around things don't ache so much. I'm maybe a little stiff, especially in the small of my back if the horses I galloped or raced yesterday pulled really hard. I've had broken ribs, fingers, my nose, toes, you name it, but I don't take any friggin' pain pills; I can get high just on aspirin so unless I get arthritis a lot worse than it is now I don't need no pills. Just a Coke and a cigarette."

Wall has been getting up in the middle of the night for most of his adult life to gallop horses, meet with trainers and hustle rides on Thoroughbreds at tracks such as Commodore Downs, Rillito Park, Tampa Bay Downs, Louisiana Downs, Waterford Park, and Prairie Meadows among other now long-forgotten tracks. For the past twenty years he has been riding the Nebraska circuit—Fonner Park, Lincoln, Columbus, and Omaha—winding down a five-decade career.

It didn't take long for Wall to leave his birthplace of Hugo, Oklahoma, and it didn't take much longer for him to abandon his next stop: a cattle ranch in the Red River Valley area of Texas on the Oklahoma border.

"Living on a farm, raising your own meat, growing your own food ... that just wasn't a life for me," says Wall, who was raised through his high school years by his grandmother in Moyers, about thirty minutes from Hugo, but spent his summers with his uncle,

Months away from his sixtieth birthday, veteran jockey Newil Wall made a riding comeback in 2006. "I didn't do it because I had anything to prove or needed any challenges, and I didn't really miss riding. Fact is, I just got bored of sitting around. I'd exercise ten or twelve horses in the morning and then do nothing all afternoon and night." Riding on the spring-summer-fall Nebraska circuit at meets sometimes lasting just a matter of days, Wall managed to ride in nearly 200 races throughout 2006 and won his share. "I wasn't top jock at any of the tracks but usually finished somewhere in mid-pack or a little better. I'm feelin' real good, my health is good, but it's still too early to decide if I want to continue riding into my 60s."

John Henry Northrip. "When my uncle left Texas to work at Ruidoso Downs in New Mexico doing maintenance work, spray painting fences and barns and all that, I tagged along. When I was in school I spent my summers at Ruidoso with my uncle, working at the track during the day and then parking cars at night. I had a few other jobs after leaving high school, but nothing to do with racing. I was 'pursuing other interests,' you might say. When I decided to go with Uncle John to Ruidoso, it didn't take much encouragement for me to begin learning all about race riding. There was a horse farm ten minutes from the track where another Texan, Nicholas S. Wolfe, had his horses broken and trained, and that's where I got started. Ridin' Quarterhorses and Thoroughbreds gave me all the excitement I was looking for. Nick Wolfe was from Giddings, just east of Austin, and was pretty big in the construction business and was also a friend and neighbor of President Lyndon Johnson. Wolfe could afford to keep quite a few horses, and after seeing me work around Ruidoso he offered me an apprentice contract, which you needed to get started in the business. Back then an apprentice, or bug boy, had to have a contract holder. A boy couldn't just walk into the racing secretary's office and ask for a jockey's license. To get a license when I broke in, it was standard to have two jockeys watch you gallop, ride or handle a Thoroughbred, and then you had to be okayed by the steward, jockeys, outriders, damned near the entire grandstand. By signing a contract with a particular owner or trainer you were locked into racing where he raced and you had to give first preference to riding his horses. Now, apprentices aren't under contract and are free to ride wherever they can get mounts, and for whoever.

"I started riding for a living in November of '69 at Rillito Park, and I did pretty well. I was leading bug boy. Of course, there was only two of us apprentices running there at the time. The circuit consisted of Tucson at the start of the year, and then on to Ruidoso, and then finished up at Albuquerque in the fall."

Wall rode the southwest circuit for a few years and then went east, riding in the Poconos, Erie, Pennsylvania, at Commodore

Downs, where he was leading rider in '74 and '75, and at Waterford Park in Chester, West Virginia, where he hooked up with Dale Baird in the mid–1970s.

"Dale was an okay guy to ride for," says Wall, "but what I really liked about riding for him was that he always had fresh horses. He might have forty head at the track and another forty at his farm getting ready for the track. And then he'd have another forty turned out for freshening or whatever. He'd have maybe 120 horses and would keep rotating stock. He always had fresher, more fit and generally sounder stock than what he was running against at Waterford. Of course, most all the races there were for $1,500 claimers with a $1,500 purse. And back then Baird would almost never buy a horse for more than $1,200 or $1,500 because it was too hard to get your money out of 'em at those low purses.

"Another angle Baird played was that if a horse was to win a cheap claimer or allowance easily, he might just take the horse off the track and send him back to the farm to let time elapse, building up eligibility for an easy condition. Baird was a condition trainer back then; probably still is. No surprise to me that he's the winningest trainer in history."

One of the more practical lessons Wall learned while bouncing around a variety of tracks early in his career is that riding the bullrings is much different from riding the larger, more upscale tracks. Bullrings are smaller-circumference, narrow tracks with tighter turns and, as a result of the confining dimensions, they offer less room to maneuver. The races at such tracks are usually shorter, 4-, 5- and 6-furlong sprints, and strategy is very important despite the seemingly one-dimensional, hell-bent for speed brevity of the races.

"Riding the small tracks is totally different from riding the larger circumference tracks," says Wall. "On a bullring the best horse may not always win. There is more strategy. Cheap speed can get out front and cut the sharp corners and hold on, especially in the four and five furlong races. Jockeys can race-ride around the tighter turns, floating a horse out or in, and that can win the race for you.

But that's just race riding—you're not trying to hurt nobody or nothing.

"Racing on the larger tracks a jock can settle into a race better, get his lane established and then when he's coming down the stretch the best horse on the day will probably win. There is nowhere near as much race riding strategy at the larger tracks. Also, at the smaller tracks the jocks tend to ride a horse a little rougher. They crouch over the horse and whup and ride, whup and ride, whipping the horse whether he needs it or not," said Wall, bending into a crouch, leaning forward over the withers of an imaginary horse and flailing first his right and then his left arm in whipping motions. "A horse can only give so much, go so fast for so long and all the whuppin' in the world ain't gonna get him home quicker. Problem is, if you don't beat on them sonsabitches you don't get to ride 'em back. The owner or trainer will figure you didn't get enough out of the horse or you weren't trying hard enough. At the larger tracks jocks and trainers seem to have a better sense of that, although there are some jocks at the major tracks that also whup and ride."

Wall didn't get too far along in his apprenticeship before he learned what he considers the number one mistake of most jockeys.

"The biggest mistake jockeys make is listening to trainers. I don't mean no disrespect by that, and I'm not puttin' trainers down. I concede that trainers know their horses better than a jock ever will, but a race has to play itself out," Wall said carefully, for years having had to choose his words deliberately so as not to offend any owners or trainers who were potentially his employers. "You can get an earful of advice in the paddock but when the gates open it's a whole new ballgame. Say, for example, you're in a race with eight horses and according to form none of them show any speed. The trainer sees there is no speed in the race and he tells you to bust out for the lead because you'll be the lone speed. Trouble is, every other trainer in the race who can read a past performance line in the *Daily Racing Form* has noticed that there is no speed in the race and he probably gave the same advice to his jockey. So, all of a sudden you've got eight horses with no speed all bustin' for the lead 'cause the trainer said so, whereas if you'da held your horse back and saved him for a late run you may have been the only closer in the race.

"I like to have a good enough relationship with a trainer so that when he asks me to evaluate a new or young horse I can tell him flat out that 'that's a piece of shit horse' without him getting' all upset and takin' me off all his other horses.

"And there's some trainers I just won't work with. I may be friendly with them away from the track, but during training hours I don't go to their barn looking for work, so there's no way of getting involved with them.

"Some of the best advice you can get in the paddock and while warming up is from the horse himself. I think they have adrenalin just like people, and they give off signals—all different, depending on the horse—when they are feeling on their game. I gotta chuckle to myself at the public perception of when a horse is going to run well. Ideally, you like to keep your horse cool and collected before a race; don't want to see him all lathered up.

"Another thing that all jockeys have to learn, and the sooner the better, is to ride a safe race. Pay attention to where you're at in the race, and to where everyone else is at. Jocks have to learn to take care of each other out there. The young riders should listen to the older riders. Younger riders are making a big mistake when they make fun of older riders because when an older rider, like me, wins a race what does that make the younger jock who finishes up the track or who got out-thought or out-maneuvered in the race?

"It can happen in the middle of a race, with the jock doing everything by the book, watching out for blind switches or horses suddenly backing up or moving out, and you can still get hurt bad but a lot of horse and jock injuries happen right in the gate, sometimes before the race even starts, when a horse might rear or bump sides of the gate.

"As a matter of fact, neither one of my two most serious injuries

III. Riders Up

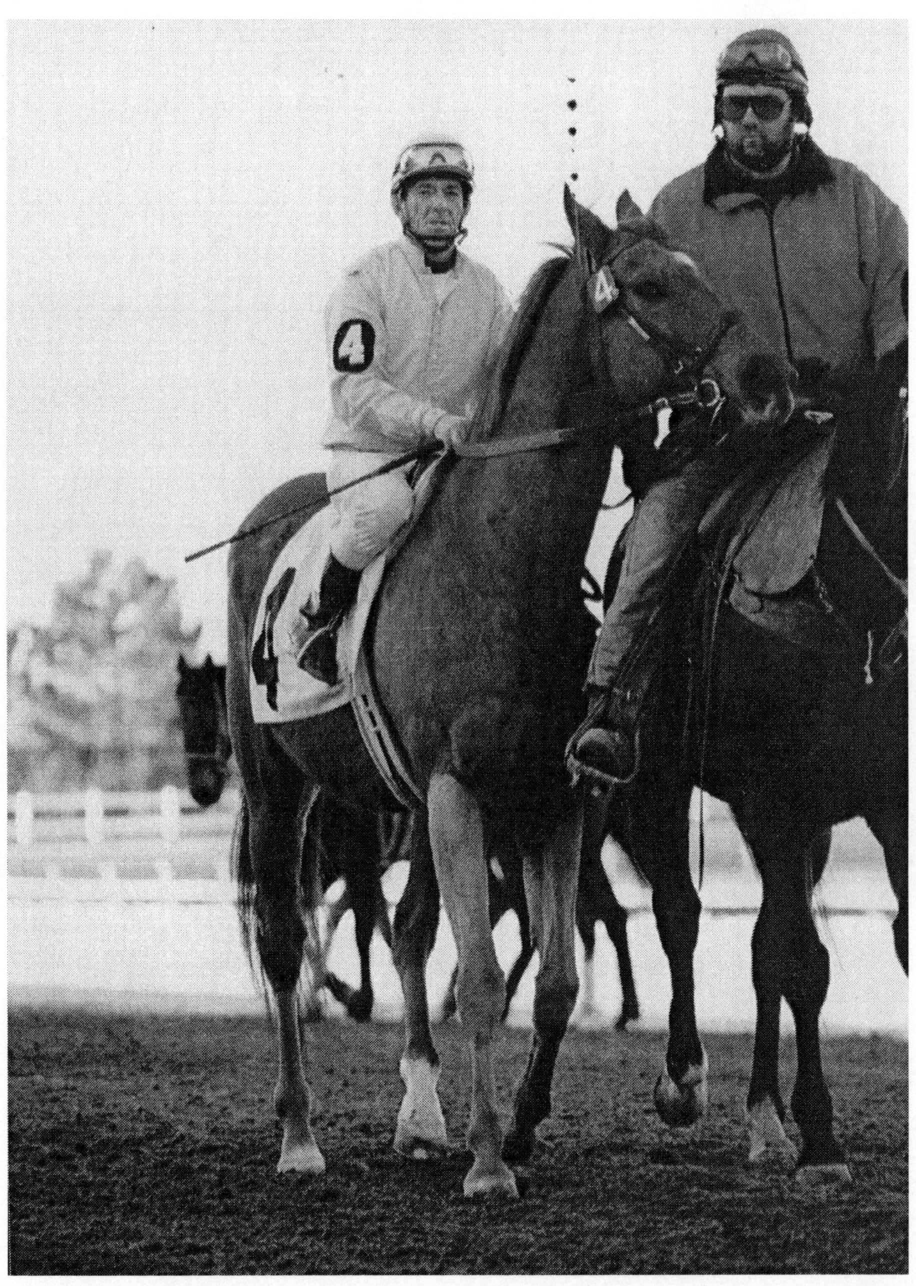

happened during a race. When I broke my right leg I was working a filly on the half-mile training track at Fonner and she was feelin' good, full of herself. When we galloped to the south side of the track there were some horses on automatic walkers. She didn't really spook, but she bobbed her head and lost her footing. When she stumbled I lost my stirrups and fell off the horse, but held onto the reins. I landed on my feet but one foot was pointed east-west and the other was north-south.

"When I broke my left leg I was in the starting gate at Lincoln, in the middle of summer and it was hotter'n hell. My horse flipped back in the gate, pinning me against the rear of the gate with the horse on top of me. I stayed fully conscious during the whole thing, but started going into shock from the heat and pain. I knew my leg was broke and I knew it was broke bad.

"When you get hurt bad and miss a lot of time, that's when true racetrackers help out and you find out your real friends. For example, about ten years ago I was the regular rider on a classy mare called Dance on the Line owned by Jack and Betty Coatney. I rode for them 14, 15 years, seven days a week as a gallop boy, breeze rider and jockey. Dance on the Line was a big, nice mare who was good right from the start of her career. In her stall she was a sweetheart; a kid could handle her, but on the track she would get hyper and was all business, always trying to work too fast. Just before one of the biggest races of her career, a big stake race at Ak-Sar-Ben here in Nebraska, I got hurt and was hospitalized for a while so lost the mount on her for the one race.

"Perry Compton, one of the leading riders around here for years,

***Opposite*: Newil Wall was the regular rider on Leaping Plum, a durable Nebraska-based gelding who accomplished an unprecedented feat by running in the same stakes race for ten consecutive years. Trained by Joe Moss, Leaping Plum raced in the 4-furlong Grasmick Handicap at Fonner Park in Grand Island, Nebraska, each year from 1995 through 2004. The speed-balling chestnut won the race 8 of the 10 times he competed, including consecutive wins from 1995 through 2001.**

replaced me as the jock on Dance and she won for fun. Later that night Perry visited me in the hospital, bringing a six pack of beer which went down real good with the morphine I was on. He also brought me $1,500, half of his winning share of the purse money....

"The injuries haven't affected the way I tactically ride a race, but I have had to make some physical adjustments. After my first serious injury when I broke my right leg I developed a tendency to drop the left stirrup lower so I could put more weight on my left—or good—leg. Then when I broke my left leg it kept me from riding with either stirrup as high as I like. For the past seven or eight years I have dropped the stirrups, riding a little longer because I can't bend my knees as much as I used to. Sometimes my knees will cramp up, and the pain in the small of my back can hurt like hell, but usually not until after the race. During the race you get naturally pumped up with a lot of adrenalin and don't feel too much.

"I'm not as strong as I used to be, which I suppose is just part of the normal aging process, and maybe partly due to an accumulation of injuries. Weight has never been a problem for me, though. I used to always ride at 110, then after I broke my leg and was inactive for a long period I could still make 115. This spring I'm kinda on sabbatical, not accepting any mounts, and my weight is 118, the most it has ever been. I'm fit enough to ride but just decided to take the spring off for no particular reason. I'm backing off and thinking about what's next for me and the family. I've been able to make a decent living here on the Nebraska circuit. The jockey fees are now $40 for a losing mount, a $5 increase over what it had been for years. Plus, you can do pretty good by just galloping horses. I usually gallop six to twelve horses a day at $10 a head, about two to two-and-a-half hours' worth of riding each morning. I like galloping horses and can't say it's difficult work unless you get a hard-puller that tries to run off. But it's easy money and by doin' that much riding you keep pretty fit. I don't suppose too many jocks get rich ridin' the Nebraska circuit, but by galloping horses and by picking up a few mounts you can make $600–$800 a week, and that pays the bills.

"I try to take one day a week off if possible, usually on a Monday or a Tuesday, which are slow workout days around here. If a trainer needs me to work a horse on my day off for an upcoming race, I'll do it. You have to oblige the trainers. Then every year Cheri and I go to Vegas for a week. I love to play blackjack and am kinda a student of the game. There's not much to do away from the track in the winter with racing shut down, so I play a lot of Internet blackjack, but just for fun, not money."

Home base for Wall is Grand Island, Nebraska, and his 40' Seaview Park travel trailer sits square on the Fonner Park grounds, a quarter mile from the track where Wall scored some of his most memorable victories. "We try to stay here in Grand Island for most of the school year so we don't have to move Kolten around from school to school. They have a good school system here and Kolten has made a lot of friends. He's active in sports and is in the band. We haven't had any problems at all with blending Kolten's schooling and life on the racetrack. Matter of fact, he learned to count before other kids his age by the colors on the horse's saddlecloths: red is 1, white is 2, blue is 3, green is 4, and so on.

"The travel trailer has been a good home for us. It's big enough for the four of us (counting Silly Girl the pig) and two air conditioners keep things cool in the summer heat. One air conditioner is for the benefit of my wife and boy, the other one is for the pig. When Fonner shuts down and I'm riding at another meet we pay $100 for someone to haul the trailer to the next track for us. We move four times a year, so for $400 a year in moving fees we get to sleep in the same beds twelve months a year. Used to be when we'd move to a different town and rent a house it would cost between $1,000–$1,500 before you even walked through the door, what with front and back-end deposits and all sorts of b.s. upfront charges that the landlord winds up screwing you out of anyway."

At 57, an age when most professional athletes have long abandoned anything more strenuous than writer's cramp at autograph shows, there is a lot more for a jockey to reflect back on than to look forward to. Wall has never been inclined toward introspection but reckons he wouldn't change much anyhow. "I can't complain," he says, recalling a career that has seen him ride in more than 10,000 races and win about ten percent of the time. "I might have done a few things different—who wouldn't?—but I have no regrets. When I finally retire I'll be ready for it. I been ridin' since 1969 and that's a long time. The last five years have kinda took a toll, what with the injuries and all. Early in my career a broken collarbone, toe, or rib was no big deal but when I broke my legs, well, that was tough to come back from.

"I've been leading rider at some tracks and that's great, but I've had some bad meets, too. Sometimes when you lose a few races you start to second-guess yourself: did you move too soon, too late, should you have gone through that small opening along the rail? When you over-think too much like that you start to lose confidence, but if you start pushing yourself or your luck too hard you hurt yourself more than help. A jock just has to realize that we all go through bad spells now and then. The big thing is puttin' food on the table. That's more important than getting your name in the *Daily Racing Form.* In the winter it's hard to eat win pictures.

"When I finally decide to retire I'm not certain what I'll be doing. I know I don't want to be a jock's agent, though some friends have asked me to take their book. I think that if I were booking mounts for a jock my sense of loyalty to him might affect my dealing with trainers. If my jock rode a good race on a particular horse and the trainer bumped him off the horse the next time the horse run for no good reason other than to use a different jock, I don't think I could deal with that diplomatically.

"I got the greatest respect for agents, but one of the few times I personally had one was some years back here in Nebraska when there weren't enough jockeys around to ride all the available mounts, and a jock could be a little choosy. I didn't have a problem getting horses to ride, but I had to hire an agent just to keep me off bad horses. I'd rather be riding an 8–1 shot than a 20–1 no-hope piece of crap, that's for sure. Most of the jocks on the Nebraska circuit have agents, though. A top jock coming here from a big-time track wouldn't have much chance at success without a good agent, no matter how good his reputation. Nowadays, an agent can make or break you."

Wall paused, tapped out a Kool, lit up and took a deep drag, slowly exhaling. He grinned.

"When I finally hang up my tack I think I'd like to go back to Oklahoma. Guess I'm just a damned Okie and I'll always be one."

10

"We rode for the love of it," or "I was tryin' to kill the son of a bitch!"

Dudley Vandenborre retired as a jockey in 1968, ending a 17-year career that played out during a period that has been frequently referred to as one of several "Golden Ages" of racing. Vandenborre rode during the tail end of an era noted for rough-and-tumble riding, lax rules, big betting coups, and Hall of Fame horses such as Citation, Native Dancer, Kelso, and Bold Ruler, many of which were ridden by arguably the most accomplished jockey of them all, Eddie Arcaro. Vandenborre rode against Arcaro and all the best of his era, winning more than 2,800 races by the time he retired.

"Yeah, I rode a lot against Arcaro," says Louisiana-born Vandenborre in a thick no-nonsense Cajun accent that audibly creates an image belying the fact that at 100 pounds he was one of the more diminutive jockeys riding. Even in his snakeskin two-inch-heel cowboy boots Vandenborre barely shades five feet. "In order to bulk myself up so my mount didn't have to carry too much weight under the saddle my wife made a special vest for me to wear. It had two pockets in the front and three in the back, and I'd put weights in the pockets to increase my weight so's the horse wouldn't have to carry too much dead weight under his saddle.

"One day in the jockey's room at one of the Chicago tracks Arcaro called me over. 'C'mere, punk,' he say and I go over—I'm just a kid and don't weigh even 100 pounds and he's a tough sonuvabitch you don't wanna mess with—and I say 'Why you call me punk, Eddie?' He said, 'Because you a bug boy. Until you win 100 races you gonna be a punk. Now, sit down and let me show you some things you doin' wrong.' And then he straddled a bench in front of the lockers and spent nearly half an hour showing me how to do things his way. How to handle the whip, how to switch hands, how to change goggles. And he was right.

"The next time I saw Arcaro I was leading apprentice at the track. He don't call me punk no more, and he was always friendly to me. That's the way it was back then. We rode for the love of it; riding was inside us. We didn't make much money, we just loved to ride and off the track we would help each other out like Arcaro helped me."

Arcaro's love of his fellow jocks had its well-documented limits, however.

Vince Nodarse, a mid-level rider who enjoyed some success in the 1940s, learned in the most literal sense that Arcaro was not to be trifled with. Shortly after the start of the 1942 Cowdin Stakes at Aqueduct, Nodarse's horse, Breezing Cool, broke sharply inward and cut off the favored Occupation, nearly putting the horse and its rider, Arcaro, over the fence. Arcaro lost his composure, flailing away at Occupation until by mid-stretch he had made up the lost ground and was running neck and neck to the outside of Breezing Cool and

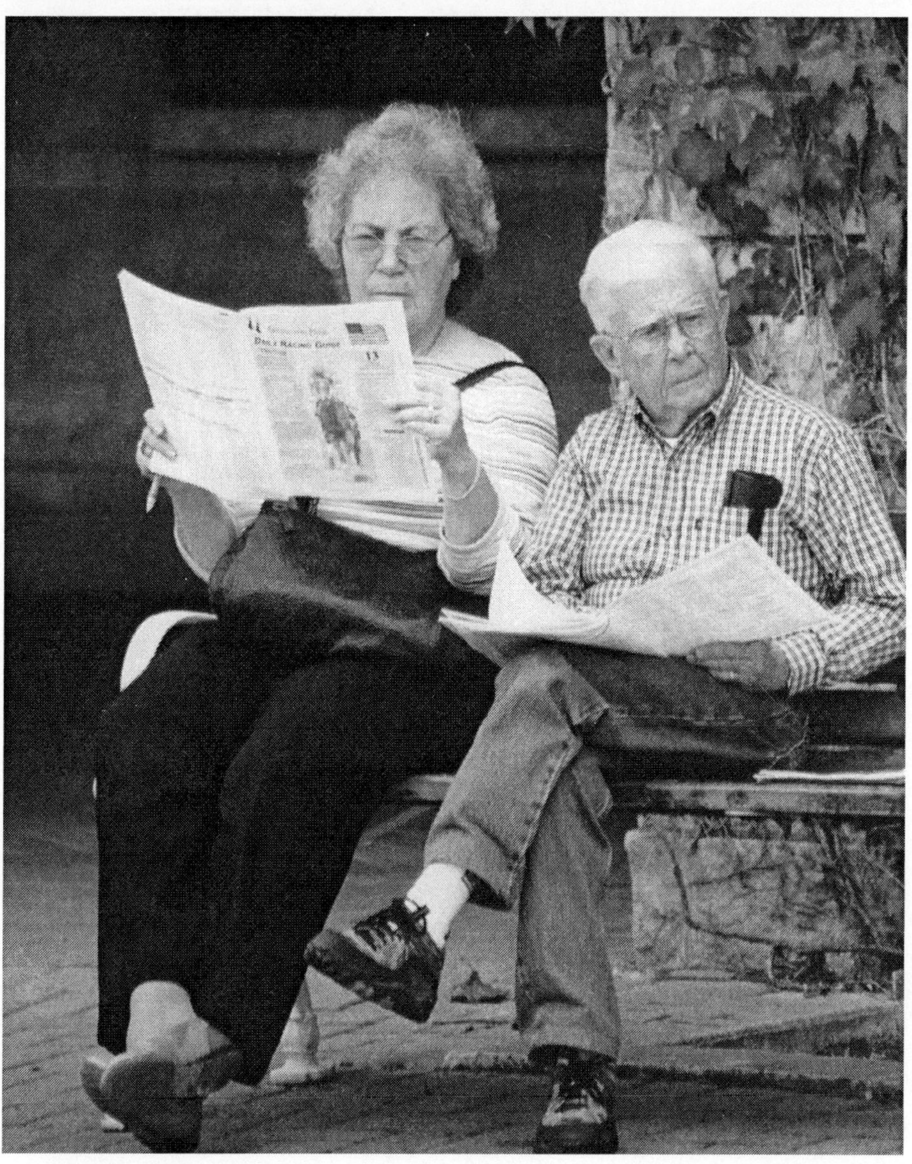

Dudley Vandenborre, shown with wife Marilyn, may have been small in stature even for a jockey but regularly rode against the most accomplished riders of his era.

Nodarse. Once he gained a slight lead, Arcaro yanked Occupation's reins to the left, cutting in front of Breezing Cool and sending Nodarse tumbling over the inner fence.

The inquiry sign went up immediately and Arcaro, still seething, could only honestly admit to the stewards when asked to explain his actions that "I was tryin' to kill the sonofabitch." As a result of his near-deadly tantrum Arcaro's license was revoked and he was suspended indefinitely, a penalty that lasted nearly a year and was lifted only when the ailing but well-connected Helen Whitney, blueblood owner of Greentree Farm, prevailed on Jockey Club chairman William Woodward, Sr., of the same social set as Mrs. Whitney. "I'd like to see Eddie Arcaro ride in my colors again before I die," she said, and a chastened Arcaro was allowed to return to the track due to Mrs. Whitney's pre-death request.

While the suspension mellowed Arcaro, he remained a physical, mental and tactical force to be dealt with and was called "the master" for good reason. Several years after the incident with Nodarse, Arcaro was riding at Keeneland in an inconsequential race on a mount that lacked the tenacity of its jockey. With his horse fading badly in the stretch, insult was added to injury when the rider on the eventual winner of the race passed Arcaro and squeezed him needlessly against the rail. The rival jockey further disrespected the master by raising up in the saddle before the finish line. Without missing a beat Arcaro reached out with his whip and lashed the offending jock across his rear, causing a two-foot-long welt. Once again appearing before the stewards, Honest Eddie said, "If it had been a tight finish I wouldn't have minded. But he was going to beat me by two anyway. He didn't need to do it." This time, according to the story as related by sportswriter Joe H. Palmer, the infraction imposed by bemused stewards was a wrist-slapping $50.

Stewards and patrol judges, located in perches high above the track to allow a panoramic furlong-by-furlong view as races developed, were able to catch most of the flagrant fouls and misdeeds but their frequently subjective scrutiny wouldn't measure up to today's video surveillance that literally scopes out every inch of the race from several angles. In the pre-video days the naked eye was assisted by racing film, which was slow to develop and limited in range. Every track had blind spots that weren't easily documented by film, and every jockey knew those dead spots and could use them to his advantage.

"Yeah, we rode because we enjoyed it, but it was a much rougher sport back then," says Vandenborre. "One of the toughest riders I ever rode against was Manny Ycaza, who rode a lot of big races in New York and Florida. He'd cut you off even if it just meant the difference between tenth and eleventh place, and he was very good at taking advantage of the blind spots on the track. But Ycaza wasn't the only one, for sure. Grabbing the bridle of a horse trying to pass you was common, along with other tricks such as locking your leg around another jock's to slow him down, hitting a rival horse or jock across the face with your whip, floating your horse in or out to impede another horse, sometimes whatever it took to get to the line first."

The horses were as tough as the jockeys, partly a result of no-nonsense training procedures that didn't coddle the Thoroughbred near as much as they are today. Horses were exercised longer and more often and they raced with greater frequency.

In November of 1968 Vandenborre was entering the starting gate of what should have been just another routine race when his mount reared, dropping the jockey heavily to the ground. The horse kicked him in the head, wheeled, and seeing the semi-conscious Vandenborre immobile and vulnerable on the ground, tried to trample him. Vandenborre survived the incident with no lasting injuries, thanks to a protective helmet that he wore as standard equipment, but his career as a jockey was over. Acceding to his wife Marilyn's wishes, Vandenborre gave up riding, spending the rest of his racetrack career as a mutual clerk at Chicago and Louisiana tracks.

One of the grittiest riders in the Midwest throughout the 1940s, '50s and '60s was Tony Skoronski, another frequent adversary of

Vandenborre's. Skoronski established his legendary small-track reputation by being able to successfully navigate the hairpin-tight turns at Sportsman's Park, which was then a half-mile bullring of a course in Cicero, Illinois, a few miles from downtown Chicago. Skoronski started riding at Sportsman's in 1942 and by the time he retired in 1969 he had won a dozen riding championships at the track as well as the nickname of "Mr. Sportsman's Park." His accomplishments become more notable when considering that Hall of Fame jockeys-to-be such as Arcaro, Johnny Longden, Bill Shoemaker, Laffit Pincay, Jr., Pat Day, Steve Brooks and Ted Atkinson at one time or another competed against Skoronski at Sportsman's.

"I rode a lot against Skoronski," says Vandenborre. "He was cocky and didn't take any crap from the fans. If he was having a bad day and the bettors got on him, he'd look right at 'em and point to his ass, and everyone knew what he meant. He was absolutely fearless riding those tight Sportsman's turns but the truth is his eyes were so bad—and he never wore glasses—he probably couldn't see good enough to be intimidated by the track. Sportsman's had the tightest turns of any track I ever rode and Tony knew that to win you had to ride hard on the turns and then rate your horse in the straightaways. If a jock was intimidated by the tight turns or just tried to cruise around them he had no shot at winning. Because of Skoronski's bad vision he had trouble reading the cards when we'd play Tonk or rummy in the jocks' room. The guys would cheat him out of his money, and then give it back. Usually."

Skoronski lived well as the perennial leading rider at Sportsman's Park and Hawthorne Race Course, but unlike a lot of contemporary jockeys who learned early to invest their money wisely as a hedge against the potentially career-ending uncertainties of the sport, Skoronski couldn't shake a strong gambling habit, and the mutual windows—as well as most card players—didn't give him his money back. The winningest rider in the Sportsman's history died broke in 1992, living out his last years in a tack room at the track.

How to Ride a Thoroughbred to the Hall of Fame

Standing ramrod-erect in the paddock, nearly immobile, arms crossed and feet slightly spread in a poster-boy pose for senior citizen jockeys, it was as though the athlete was a rooted stake driven into the ground with a mallet. At first only the jockey's shiny dark eyes moved, vertically shifting from the saddling stall of his mount in the upcoming race and then back to the ground. Occasionally he would cross and uncross his arms, twirl his whip and then slap it against the side of his riding boot. Earlie Fires was not nervous; he had stood in this or similar paddocks tens of thousands of times. It was just a matter of impatient anxiety. When the trainer finished his saddling chores, first placing a moist chamois on the horse's back followed by foam saddle pads, a saddle towel, the saddle and rubber girth channels to prevent the girth straps from rubbing the horse's belly, then the under-girth straps, the over-girth straps, a tongue-tie to keep the horse from swallowing his tongue—after all this procedural routine, the trainer would then finally turn to meet with the jockey, perhaps to give last-minute instructions or a light-hearted tension-breaking comment such as, "Ride him like you stole him," or simply, "Have a safe trip." Sometimes, particularly in important races, the horse's owner would approach Fires to introduce family members or friends to the weathered, fifty-eight-year-old Hall of Fame rider. Unfailingly polite to owners and outwardly receptive to trainers, Fires didn't reveal any telltale signs of impatience but he was anxious to get on with the race. In the twilight stage of an outstanding career, Fires now rode solely because he enjoyed it; he liked to go fast on a horse and he liked to compete. It was what he knew best.

Born and raised on a farm in Rivervale, Arkansas, forty miles outside of Memphis, Earlie Fires was one of eleven children. After working the family cotton, soybean and wheat fields as a youth—and learning to ride a horse after the chores were done—Fires tried the amateur rodeo circuit with mixed success. Eventually he worked his way to Arlington Park, where, at 15, he worked as an exercise rider for trainer Harold "Baldy" Tinker. From Tinker he went to work for Willard Proctor, who put him under contract and gave him his first chance to ride. Fires rode his maiden winner on March 6, 1965, at Oaklawn Park, followed by two hundred and twenty-three more winners during the year, making Fires the nation's leading apprentice. His career stayed in high gear, winning his first $100,000 stakes race less than a year later. Sixteen years later he won his 3,000th race. Win number 6,000 came in another sixteen years, in 1998. He was officially added to the roster of Thoroughbred racing's all-time greats when he was elected to the National Museum of Racing and Hall of Fame in 2001. In 2002 he was added to the Walk of Fame in his home state of Arkansas, joining, among others, racing's Pat Day and Larry Snyder, baseball's Dizzy Dean and Brooks Robinson, musicians Johnny Cash and Glen Campbell, movie star Alan Ladd, military hero General

Douglas MacArthur, and President William Clinton. In 1991 Fires received the George Woolf Memorial Jockey Award, presented annually by Santa Anita Park to a North American jockey who demonstrates high standards of personal and professional conduct, both on and off the track.

Fires has won riding championships at Arlington Park, Hawthorne Race Course, Hialeah Park, Calder Race Course, Keeneland, Churchill Downs, Gulfstream Park and Miles Park.

Fires' work day had started a little more than an hour before he was due in the paddock. Wheeling his Jeep Cherokee into the restricted parking area adjacent to the jockey's quarters, it took the popular rider several minutes to wend his way through the banter and greetings of attendants and security guards. Once inside, Fires bypassed the table tennis, pool table and other recreational diversions and headed straight for the hot box. To make his usual weight of 116, Fires would have to sweat off the excess pounds from a muscular, near fat-free frame, slightly shorter in stature than the average jockey, that had been gained since yesterday's races. As were all riders at Arlington Park, Fires was required to be in the jockey's quarters an hour before his first mount. For many jocks the day started much earlier as they curried favor with trainers by exercising various Thoroughbreds during the 5:30 A.M. to 10:15 A.M. hours when the main track was open for training. Nearing the end of his career, Fires seldom got out at daybreak to exercise a horse. "Ninety-five percent of the riders get on from one to five, six horses every morning, every day of the week. I used to do all that, and occasionally I'll still work a horse, but not too often any more," says Fires. Not working horses in the morning meant that he had to sweat off pounds in the afternoon.

"Most of us guys [jockeys] have to come in and take off the overnight weight. Say for instance you been out and had a few drinks, a couple of beers. Sometimes that weight don't come off too easy, especially if you're not exercising horses in the morning. You have to hit the steam room or work out in other ways to get that weight

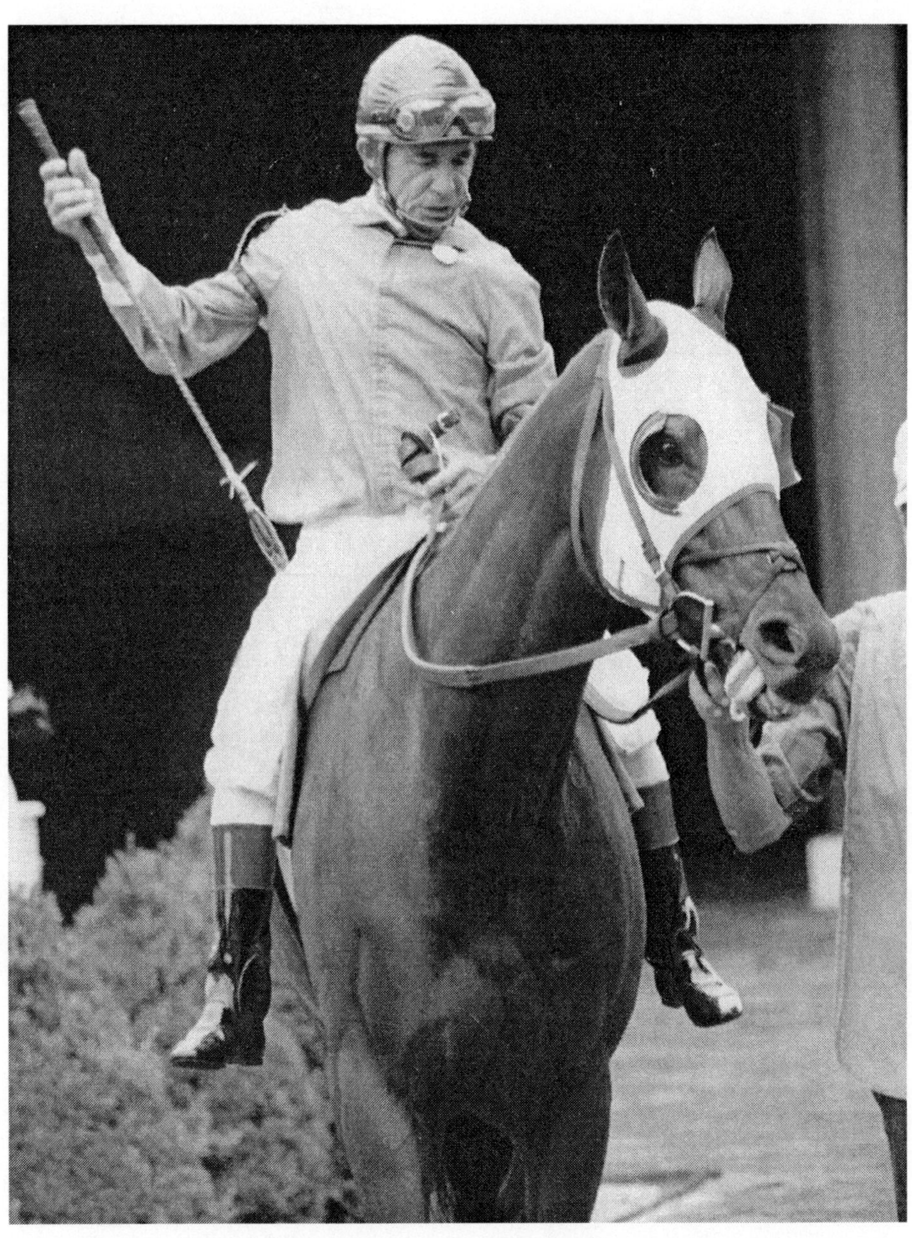

Earlie Fires transforms into a Hall of Fame jockey the instant he gets a leg up on a horse. The way his feet dangle out of the stirrups, the manner of holding the reins and whip, is all purposeful.

off. Besides our actual weight we are carrying an extra four pounds because of a required protective safety jacket and helmet but that weight don't count against your assigned weight.

"So, we get here maybe an hour before our first race, work out or hit the steam box. About fourteen minutes before post-time the paddock judge calls us out to the paddock. The time can vary a little depending on what's going on in the paddock. Once we're in the paddock the trainer will usually—but not always—give some instructions. Sometimes the instructions are good; the trainer might warn you that a horse will tend to lug in or out, or have other quirky habits. Sometimes instructions don't work out. Say a trainer tells you to take your horse back 'cause he don't like to be close up and you go a half in :51 or :52. That puts you back a ways in the race and if all the other horses are running near the lead you can't make up no ground. It looks like your horse run a bad race but he run just as good a race as the other horses. His chance to win was taken away from him is all.

"But generally we're hired to ride a horse the way the trainer wants it ridden. Maybe seventy percent of trainers really don't give you instructions, or at least don't expect you to hold to the instructions if the race comes up different from what's expected. The other thirty percent of the trainers out there feel if you don't ride to suit them, win or lose, you're fired.

"A trainer is not on the track ridin' the race. They can't see if you're getting' blocked, they don't know if your horse is responding that day, they don't know a lot of things. They don't know if a horse stumbled leaving the gate, hit the side of the gate, they can't see a lot of things that happen. A good trainer will ask how a race played out. There's a million ways out there to get beat."

At the call for riders up, Fires is boosted onto his mount, leaving his feet out of the stirrups, dangling at the side of the horse.

"You should let your feet dangle but a lot of riders get up and put their feet right in the stirrups. Different riders have different ways. Me, I keep my feet out until I tie the knot in the reins so if the horse does rear or lunges I can stay with him. Most of the time if you got your feet in the stirrups while you're tying your knot, if he jumps he'll jump out from under you.

"There's a lot of little things a rider should learn about getting on a horse. For example, if a horse is a little shy of the whip they should learn to put their stick in their left hand and put it up by the mane and then jump up on the horse instead of throwing the stick up over their head. But you can't tell a lot of today's riders anything. 'Aw, you ride your horse and I'll ride mine,' they say. Years ago kids would listen to older jocks but no more. Same as it is with the whole world. There's a whole different group of kids out there now, same as there is in everyday life."

Years ago young riders had to be under exclusive contract to experienced trainers or owners, but that wasn't a good thing, says Fires. "Sometimes a trainer would put two or three kids under contract as an apprentice jockey and just use them for cheap labor, like exercise boys, for four years [the duration of the contract] and retard their development as a rider. Now we got a certificate system. You give a trainer your certificate to hold but if you want it back you can get it, which works out a lot better. What I have a problem with now, and so do most experienced riders, is that most young jocks don't want to learn the basics before they start; they want to learn to ride by riding. And we can't do a thing about it because we got so many kids coming from other countries now and they claim they've been in riding schools and everything else in their home country. [Hall of Fame ex-jockey] Chris McCarron's idea for a riding school in Kentucky is absolutely a great idea. I'm 100% for it."

Once boosted into the saddle Fires ties a knot in the reins.

"You hold the reins all like a half-cross almost all the time you're on a horse." [A cross occurs when the rider pulls the reins toward him, together at the back of the horse's neck. If the reins are held in both hands, it's a full cross. A half cross occurs when the rider holds both reins in one hand, as when changing whip hands or to cock the whip or for whatever other reason. When the horse is galloping most riders will use a full cross. A rider will throw a cross when acceleration is desired, essentially shortening the reins and tugging at the bit in the horse's mouth. Early in training a horse is taught to pull on the bit, and throwing a cross can be the signal for the horse to pull, or accelerate.] As Fires says, "You throw the reins together and then you got a cross. You just got your hand, your little finger, on the outside of the reins. Actually you're only holding with three fingers, and some guys you see holding with two fingers, especially when they're riding. You may not see them in the walking ring holding with two fingers but I see them finishing sometimes with only two fingers on the reins.

"During a race sometimes a rider will throw a cross, shaking the horse's bit, to make the horse run a little. Some horses react to that. But when you're just walking a horse in the paddock you got to take a longer hold. Maybe you got a half cross and a hand full of mane in case the horse gets spooked and tries to lunge out from under you or something.

"After we break out of the post parade we really need about six minutes to get our horses warmed up, and it's a time when you can get familiar with your horse. Every horse you ride feels a little different, so sometimes your feet are up or down on one side or another and you try to get adjusted. Sometimes you get on a skinny horse. If you've been riding bigger horses you may have to raise both sides of your stirrups one or two holes to make yourself feel as comfortable as you was on the bigger horses. It means a lot how your legs feel when you stand up on a horse, and you usually get that checked out during the six-minute warm-up time before you get to the gate. Eighty percent of the horses you don't really change much on them. But there is the small percent of horses that you put one notch on the right or maybe on the left side or maybe on both sides. Sometimes it's two or three notches if you're on a real skinny horse. When you see a rider pull his leg out and fold it up during the warm-up it means they don't feel comfortable with that particular horse." Fires has made few stylistic riding changes due to age or injury.

"When I first started riding I rode short (with the stirrups close to the saddle) and then I had one of my regular trainers to tell me I was ridin' too short. So then I rode short on the left side and kept the right longer, like Bobby Baird and a few other jocks around here. Then another trainer would tell me I was ridin' too long. Gets so you feel like a seesaw. Now if a jock asks me about settin' the stirrups I just tell them to ride the best way you feel comfortable. Don't change your style because somebody else is telling you ... unless of course you see some apprentice guy falling off his horse all the time. Then you gotta suggest that they do something different. But being comfortable on a horse is the most important thing.

"When I broke my left leg a while back I had to raise the left stirrup a little higher. For about two months I could barely put pressure on my left leg and I was riding mostly on my right leg. By keeping my sore leg higher up I was able to put most of the pressure on the other leg. Riders don't really ride in their stirrups as hard as people think they do anyway, so changing my left stirrup didn't throw off my balance none. We ride pretty light in our stirrups and just balance on the horse. You get comfortable, get balanced, and try to stay that way. You don't really push down hard in the stirrups."

Fires considers his reputation as a speed jockey—a discernment earned through bettors regularly seeing his horse on the lead—undeserved, but does feel he gets his mounts out of the gate in good order.

"I don't consider myself a speed rider, but I am a good gate rider. The important thing in the gate is to get the horse set good. Just place him good, that's all, standing square on their feet. And the guy in the gate with you is important in helping get your horse set straight. Here at Arlington this guy Bill Knott is the best starter I've ridden under in my forty years of riding. He lets every rider, every gate man know where he's at in the gate. If your horse is sittin' messed up just let the starter know and he'll wait. And then just before he opens the gates he lets you know he's going to shoot the gun."

Many jockeys feel that if a horse is reluctant to load into the gate it may be because the horse is a little sore. The theory is that Thoroughbreds are smart enough to know that they will be racing when they leave the gate and that it will be strenuous and probably hurt. They anticipate the pain and therefore are hesitant to load. A cursory glance at any program will reveal that most horses run on Lasix (Salix) or butezolidin, pharmaceutical agents that enable a horse to run less pain-inhibited. The good horses run fast enough to have or generate problems; slow horses don't usually run hard enough to get hurt. As horses age, many will wise up and slow down as a self-protective device, a concession which can cause a rapid descent into the claiming ranks or other low-quality races.

"I am also a good pace rider," Fires continued. "If the pace is too slow I am going to make it go decent enough. I have been considered a speed rider but if you see me on the front end it's because there isn't any pace in the race. If there is pace in the race I'll be further back. That's how you should ride a race. People say 'Get Earlie Fires if you want a good front end rider' but I'm only gonna be there if the pace is too slow. I used to ride a lot against Pat Day when he run at Arlington and I've seen him win a jillion races on the lead but he was considered a sit-still jockey. Yeah, he sit still on the front."

Before becoming Arlington Park's all-time leading rider with more than 2,800 wins at the track (and six riding championships), Fires regularly rode in Kentucky, where he won numerous Keeneland spring and fall riding championships. "I rode in Kentucky for years until my kids started school and then I had to quit that circuit. I used to go to Keeneland and Churchill in the spring and fall and was leading rider many times, but I just couldn't handle it with the kids in school in Chicago. You have to give your kids a shot in life, too. I liked Kentucky but I love Arlington Park better than any racetrack I've ever been to in my life. I rode Hialeah during the winter months and that was a beautiful track. Rode it from '65 until it closed down a few years back."

Once the gate opens the real riding starts.

III. Riders Up

"Hardly any rider takes a cross in the gate because actually what they do is put a hand on each rein, and get a handful of mane in each hand, too. So you got a rein and a handful of mane in each hand so if a horse ducks one way or another the jock knows which way to correct them and just keep on riding the horse without an interruption. For example, if a horse ducks in, you can turn loose of that hand and straighten up your horse and keep lettin' him run. So then after you got him running straight you can throw a half cross and ride them from there. It could be a long cross or it could be a short cross, depending on how the rider feels on the horse or according to the horse. Might be a high-headed horse or a horse that runs with his head low to the ground. Horses don't carry their heads the same. Believe me, they're all different.

"Sometimes the trainer can tell the jock how a horse holds his head or whatever, but usually, unless it's a new horse, we already know how a horse carries his head, or breaks from the gate. The riders share little things about a horse that might keep us from getting hurt. Not all the guys share that information, but most do.

"So when you're in the gate you're actually sitting down on the horse and when they leave there you just kinda grab the mane and raise up and stay off of their mouth (keep from pulling too hard on the reins). Some guys do crouch down and lean a little forward, but that's all what's to your liking and how you feel comfortable on a horse. Then, you try to stay that way, being still, on the horse all the way around the track."

Approaching 60, Fires is still able to get low on a horse, knees bent, back parallel, coffee-table flat, head tucked behind the horse's neck, an aerodynamically desirable position as well as aesthetically attractive.

"Well," says Fires, "nowadays everybody seems to be floppin' around, floppin' their arms, just kinda showboatin'. Well, maybe not really showboatin', I guess it's just their style. I suppose looking good and level on a horse just looks good in the win picture.

"Bill Hartack [a Hall of Fame jockey who won five Kentucky

Derbies] never looked good on a horse. He looked like he was bouncin' but he really wasn't. He just had a little awkward way of riding. Everybody thought he looked bad, but he just kinda had a little wobble to his style, maybe because he hit left-handed. He was left-handed so he had a wobble way of moving. He could hit right-handed but most of the time he hit left-handed. I rode with Bill for a long time. Bill was a good rider. He was a clean rider and an intelligent rider. He was smart in what he was doing."

With retirement still somewhere in the future, Earlie Fires has won more than 6,300 races. Bill Hartack retired with 4,272 wins. Other Hall of Fame jockeys and their win totals include Johnny Longden (6,032); Jerry Bailey (5,893); Jacinto Vasquez (5,231); Eddie Arcaro (4,779); Gary Stevens (5,005); Don Brumfield (4,573); Steve Brooks (4,451); Eddie Maple (4,398); and Walter Blum (4,382). Today's leading riders, Edgar Prado and John Velazquez, each have fewer wins than Fires, which is natural since they began their careers at a much later date.

"When you change your stick hand [switching from left to right or vice-versa] you have to change reins," says Fires. "Now, most riders can shift right-handed or left-handed. Some guys can do it in a snap of a finger; some guys it takes a little bit longer. But that comes from riding a lot. Just like developing a sense of pace. Knowing how fast you're going is what separates successful riders from unsuccessful riders. You have to have a sense of how fast you're going and of how fast the other horses are going. You can't actually count out the time between poles because you got too much else to think about ... you just have to have a sense of pace. It takes a lot of practice, and some natural skill, to be a winning rider. When you're starting out and you're not riding enough horses you don't have that rhythm of being able to change and cross and move real good. But if you start riding three, four, five horses a day then the rhythm comes. Then you can get a feel for pace, switch sticks, goggles, whatever. I wear four sets of goggles all the time. Going a mile and an eighth I wear

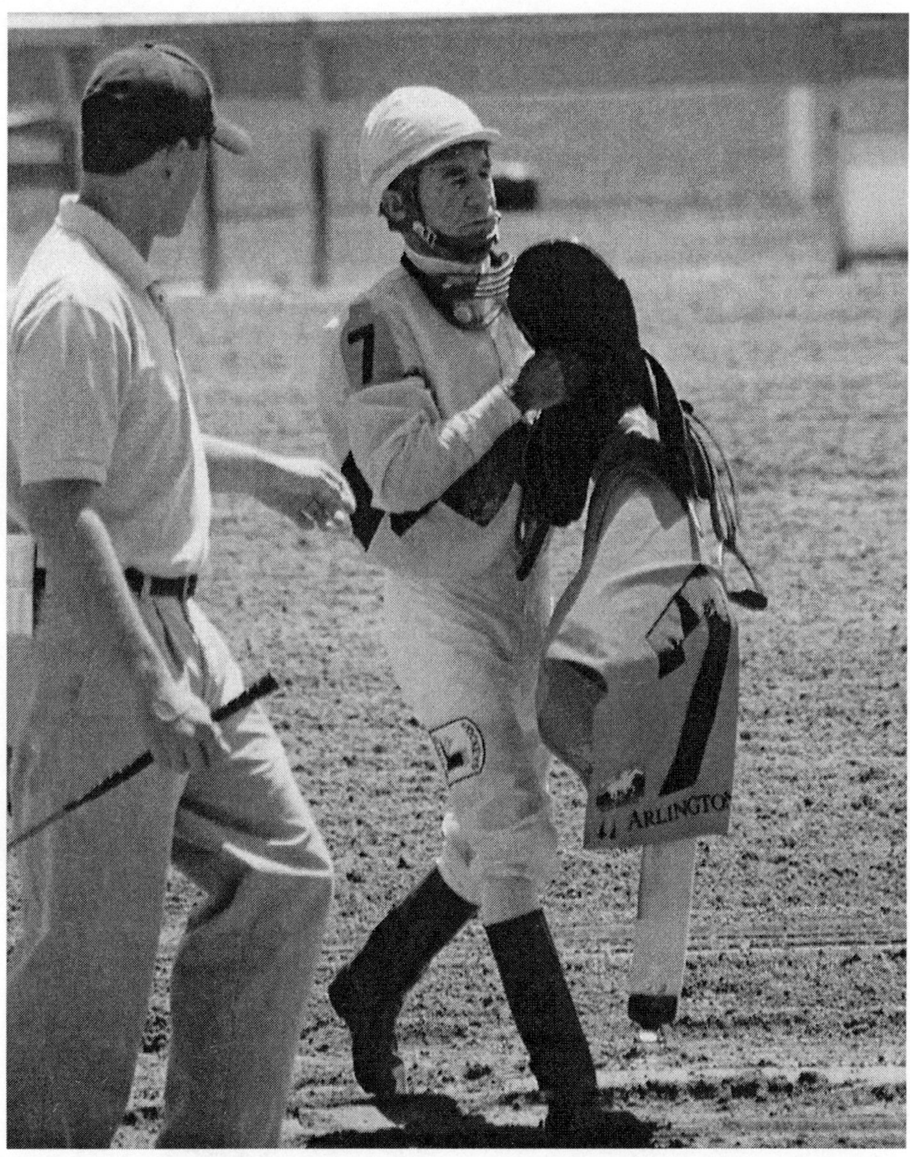

As a matter of routine a jockey must weigh in immediately after a race in order to confirm that he rode and finished with the correct, assigned amount of weight.

five. If the track is real muddy I might wear six. That's one of the reasons jocks are apprentices for a year when they're just starting out. They learn all the basics and develop timing and that's what gives them at least the opportunity to become a top rider.

"Getting a horse to change leads is usually a pretty natural thing for a horse if they've been taught in the morning, during training. But basically, when you go into the turn during a race a lot of jocks want to pull a horse in going through the turn. Actually, what you do, you turn them out because when you turn their head out a little bit they'll turn in. You don't wheel them out, you just turn their head a little bit to the right and they switch over to their left lead and go around the turn.

"It's different in the stretch. You're not really trying to get them to change leads in the stretch, you're trying to get them straight. Probably seventy percent of the horses change automatically because they've been taught in the morning. But then you get some of them that you don't ever make them change. And if they're running good on that lead why make them do it any other way? If they're still strong why mess with them? But if I am coming down through the stretch and I think a horse might beat me and my horse might do better if he changes leads, then I'll try to make him change leads 'cause I'm thinking he might give me that little extra. But it ain't just me that does it; all the riders do the same thing.

"Horses don't necessarily change leads 'cause they're getting tired or going in and out of turns. It's just something that's been taught to them from the day they were babies. If they're not doing it then I'll tell you somebody has done a bad job of training.

"You can usually tell when a horse is changing leads. When you're coming down the stretch and the horse is getting a little late on you and hasn't changed leads yet, the rider tries to do something. Some horses automatically want to make the change. Some trainers will tell you that 'This horse is lazy about changing leads so if you can make him change leads he'll give you a little extra.' That's the type of good trainer instruction in the paddock that helps.

III. Riders Up

"Riding a horse on turf is a lot different than on the dirt. I love the grass. You never have to pull goggles down, your horse is never checking like they do running into the dirt. I think turf horses run more honest every race. If the horse figures to do such and such a thing he'll probably do it unless he bled or something. It's not because he got hurt by dirt or because you got stuck nine wide trying to get your horse out of the dirt. On the turf you can tuck them in without much problem. Saving ground is important in turf races. In dirt races a lotta horses don't like getting hit in the face with dirt so you have to take them wide. In dirt races if you could sit on the inside and then wheel out you could win a lot of races. But most of the time when you're on the inside in a dirt race you're the second horse out and still getting hit by dirt.

"Some people have also called me a whip rider. Well, using the whip should actually be the last resort to motivate a horse, if you really want to know the truth. Basically the rider will just tap a horse on the shoulder way before he hits him. You don't whip him on the shoulder, you just tap the horse and basically that's what everybody does leaving the starting gate. The tap is the first thing that riders are trying to get the horse to run from. Just tap them on the shoulder, then some riders might raise up a little and show the stick to the horse and hope they'll run from that. Then you're hand riding and tapping on the shoulder and the last resort is having to hit the horse. A rider may show the horse the stick before he hits him because riders really don't like hitting the horse. I want to just run off with the win without whipping, if you want to know the truth. I always want to not have to use the whip. But I got this reputation because I got put on a lot of horses that the owners and trainers knew needed ... encouragement. Let's call it encouragement.

"I've seen some jocks break I don't know how many sticks in the past few years. Maybe they're using limber whips or something. I don't think I've broke a whip in maybe ten years. The poppers wear out and stuff like that but that's about all. Sometimes you might go to hit your horse and hit the rail instead and break your whip. A whip is kinda like a fishing rod. You pull too hard on the rod with a big fish on the end it's gonna snap. Some jocks hit harder than others; they say the horse runs better, but I don't know about that. In the heat of battle sometimes a rider can get carried away with the stick....

"The ridin' don't stop when you pass the finish line, though. You got to let your horse run out, gallop another couple furlongs or so to prevent him cramping up. Then after you gradually slow him down you just turn him around and slowly walk or jog him to the grandstand area ... and hopefully the winner's circle.

"It probably helps to know a horse's peculiarities but now I just ride a horse basically the way the trainer says. Fifteen years ago I might not know the horse's actual name but I would remember him as soon as I got on his back. As I got older I kinda lost a little bit of that but for the last fifteen years up until about three years ago I was doing just as good without knowing all that. But now that I decided to slow up a little bit with my number of mounts it's cost me a lot of business. When you quit riding as much the trainers quit using you as much. If you don't ride their slow horses they ain't gonna put you on the fast ones. When you try to semi-retire in this business, well, there just ain't no such thing. You either ride or you retire. Craig Perret is a good example of that. He don't want to ride cheap horses no more. He just wants to ride allowance or stakes horses and that has hurt his business big time.

"I never really had a goal like being the country's leading rider, but if it happened I sure took it. But I always take off a month or two every year, so I never really got hungry for records or titles. In '65 I was the leading apprentice in the country [with 224 wins], and then I was second or third in the country several times. I think the most I win in a year was about 300 races [Fires has won five riding titles at Arlington Park, five at Keeneland, four at Churchill Downs, three at Hawthorne, and single riding titles at Gulfstream Park, Hialeah and Calder. He twice won seven races on one program at Arlington and once won six out of six races at Hawthorne].

"Back when I was starting out and really going good we used to run six days a week, but we didn't run at night. A few years later, when night racing started up, some younger riders would ride day and night, guys like Chris McCarron and Kent Desormeaux, and that's how they wind up winning 500–600 races as apprentices. I wouldn't want to go at that pace anyway. You have no family life and the pace would beat you into the ground. 'Course, many of those younger riders actually like the competition, but I was brought up to know there's enough money out there for us all. And I ain't never been greedy in that way.

"Now that I'm getting a little older I have had to let up a little bit. I used to ride a horse a lot harder, but a lot of riders rode that way when I started out. Now the animal rights people have everybody concerned so I kinda had to slack off. It hurt my business a bit 'cause other riders were riding harder, whipping their horses harder than me.

"I feel as strong as ever, though. I'm fit, so my conditioning's not the reason my business has slacked off. Whatever, I'm riding a lot less than I used to. I don't think I'd really like to ride much more than I do now, three or four a day, but I would like to ride a better quality of horse. I could ride 300 or more head of horses a year, but I'll probably get on maybe 250. That's more than enough mounts but I'd like to be on better horses."

Fires' top stakes horses include In Reality, Abe's Hope, Foolish Pleasure, War Censor, Swinging Mood, Pattee Canyon, Classy Cathy, Tumble Wind and One Dreamer.

Running Hard, Going Slow

The first day of each January all Thoroughbreds share a universal birthday and are officially considered a year older. Yearlings become two-year-olds and will soon be leaving familiar childhood pastureland to begin preparation for their initiation into the demanding world of the race course. Two-year-olds have turned three and many have already seen action at the track: some have shown promise and a very elite few will be pointed toward racing's classic series of the Kentucky Derby, the Preakness, and the Belmont Stakes. Others will be running in claiming races, available for purchase, to become someone else's dream or to simply help fill out a workaday stable roster.

Some of the horses on the market will be bought or sold by Dan Arrigo, who still daily patrols tracks on the Internet, looking to pluck a potential broodmare from a claiming race with the intention of giving her a home in somebody's breeding shed. The past year had been a bit unusual for Arrigo. "I probably sold fewer horses than in most previous years," he shrugged, "but my dollar volume was up. The market was strong; I had to overpay for almost everything I bought but everything I bought also sold well." He had not handled any graded stakes horses throughout the year but several maiden mares he sold in previous years produced graded stakes horses. Finishing up the year with flourish, Arrigo's annual pickle sale in the Hawthorne Race Course paddock grossed $72,650 on the sale of thirty-three horses, an average of slightly more than $2,200 per horse. Forty had been entered. Freedom's Answer, a three-year-old Illinois-bred gelding by Mutakddim who remained a maiden after nine starts at various Illinois tracks, topped the sale with a bid of $10,000, selling to Dale Baird, one of ten he purchased at the sale.

On February 24, opening day at Hawthorne Race Course's 2006 spring meet, Arrigo and two partners claimed a 4-year-old gelding from a $5,000 claiming race with the intention of keeping him in training. For Arrigo the cycle of managing and training a small stable would start all over again.

Baird, the leading buyer at Arrigo's auction, did customarily well throughout 2005 while continuing to race almost exclusively at Mountaineer Park. The prolific trainer padded his world record win total by 167 and added more than $2 million in purse money, ranking him number eleven in wins and 64th in money earned. As an owner Baird ranked third in wins with 159 and 25th in money earned for the year. Continuing just as consistently in 2006, by the end of September he was nearing 9,300 wins and $33,000,000 in lifetime earnings.

Midwest-based trainer Ralph Martinez continued his upwardly spiraling quest for wins, purse money and national recognition in 2005 by winning 194 races in his capacity as private trainer for Louis O'Brien's Shamrock Stable. Martinez ranked 6th nationally in races won for the third consecutive year, ahead of marquee trainers such as Bill Mott, Wayne Lukas, Bob Baffert and Bobby Frankel.

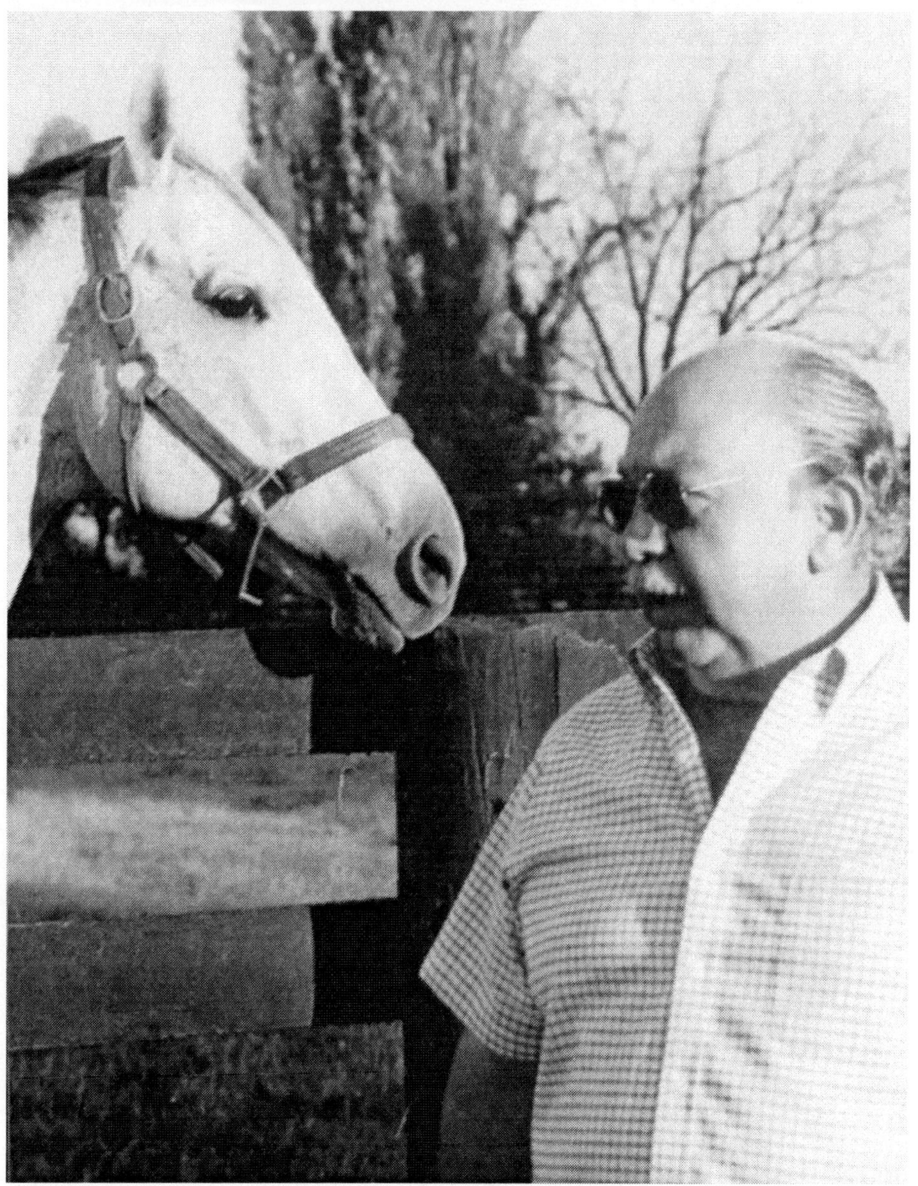

Dan Arrigo with 1998 Horse of the Year Skip Away at Rick Trontz's Hopewell Farm in Midway, Kentucky.

Performing more like a white shark in a rubber wading pool than merely a big fish in a small pond, Martinez was the leading trainer at every track at which he ran regularly: Hoosier Park, Indiana Downs, Fairmount Park. It was Martinez's third consecutive training title at Hoosier Park and maintained his astonishing record of having won the trainer's title at every meet at every track at which he stabled a full complement of horses. O'Brien again finished second nationally in number of wins by an owner, and was the leading owner at every track at which Shamrock Stables regularly raced.

At Mole Meadows, the farm's first homebred Thoroughbred, Are You Dancing, reached juvenile racing age and owner Morgan McDonnell remained buoyant. "She's growing into a real lady," he said. "Her chest has widened, her legs are straight and she has responded positively to all of her early training. We have been able to work with her through the winter months at a nearby state-of-the-art indoor private training facility formerly operated by Olympic Equestrian silver medalist Chris Kappler." The 60' by 120', seven-stall facility proved an ideal initiation to breaking and training. "The filly did so well lunging and accepting her long line training that on the third day of working with her, my 12-year-old daughter handled the lines," said McDonnell. "I had no problems, aside from a little bucking, getting on Dancing's back using an English saddle, being led, and several sessions without being led. She is a very serious horse with the mannerisms of an old broodmare and she is very focused on her training. After a few more weeks of repetitive work we'll turn her out for three months, until spring, just to let her mature. I had planned to ship Are You Dancing to Florida, to a farm recommended by Billy Turner, for her final racetrack preparations but the winter weather was so mild in northern Illinois this year that we just kept her here.

"Our other foal, Captain Fluffy, is large for a just-turned-yearling. Her rump must be 5'6" or so, and she is correct in every way. She's going to be a huge filly. It's too early for any actual serious training but we handle her a lot, picking up her feet, breaking her to a halter. We are still teaching her manners; she's going to have to learn to behave because she is so strong. We used a less stressful, less conventional form of weaning with her and it worked well. The concept involves separating her from her dam by putting them in separate but adjacent fields where they can run up to each other, rub noses and talk. After a day or so they each more-or-less went their own ways. The weaning process works best if you have several other horses in each paddock to occupy the attention of the mare and foal. Overall I am so pleased with Fluffy that I am sending her dam back to Chicago Six this spring."

Newil Wall didn't accept any mounts throughout the year but maintained that he hadn't retired. "I'm just taking some time off," said Wall of his riding career. "My health is okay. I put on four or five pounds but can still tack out at 118, 119. I get up on horses in the morning and make ten dollars a head by galloping, which is more than I can make as a track official. I'm still not gettin' rich but the four hundred or so that I pull down every week pays the bills. Because I follow the Nebraska racing circuit around galloping horses, I am able to spend a lot of time with my family. My wife, Cheri, recently took a job with a local bank, which means we have good insurance benefits. I don't know if I'll ride again, but I know I'm not officially retired yet."

In Louisiana, Dudley Vandenborre and his wife, Marilyn, continued to enjoy retirement, thankful that killer hurricanes Katrina and Rita had not caused any personal injuries or irreparable damage to their home fifteen miles northeast of New Orleans. For Earlie Fires, 2005 was about as bad as it could get. His wife of 36 years, Kathy, died in early fall after a lingering illness. After taking several months off to put his thoughts and life together, Fires eventually accepted a few mounts at the Hawthorne winter meet and then took off near the end of the year to go on his annual skiing vacation and prepare for the Gulfstream meet. On February 3 at Gulfstream, riding 5–1 shot Royal Master in a seven-furlong claiming race, Fires broke well, held his horse off the pace for the first quarter and then

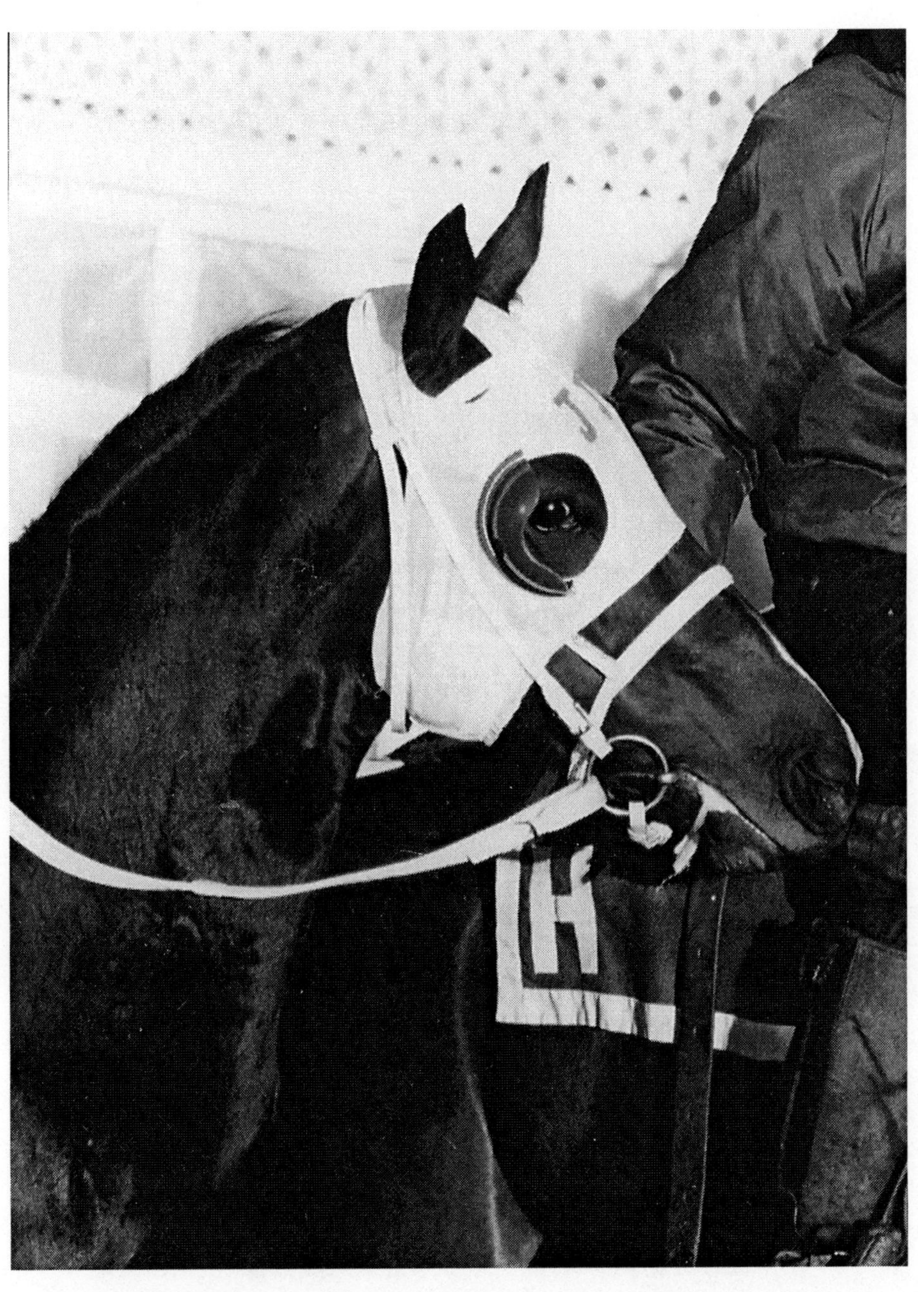

Call Me Loverboy, the handsomest horse on the track from the knees up.

made a big move around the final turn to win going away by three-quarters of a length, posting his first win of the year. With just a month to go before his 59th birthday, there still "wasn't nothing" he'd rather be doing, which he showed when he returned to riding fulltime at Arlington's spring meet.

The Betting People were given a new arena at which to play, Zia Park in Hobbs, New Mexico, a one-mile track hard on the Texas border. Most players would only see the inside of it through the glass screen of a simulcast television monitor, but so what? It had a starting gate, a finish line and an odds board. And horses. And it also had, to start, 690 slot machines, meaning that the Betting People would share the facility with the Gambling People.

But the storybook, just-won-the-lottery ending goes to the hard-trying, injury-prone tough guy with the soft, rubbery lips, Call Me Loverboy. He had won three of his final four races despite the persistence of ankle and knee problems that could have eventually proved fatal, when trainer and co-owner Arrigo retired Loverboy rather than risk a calamitous injury. The mahogany bay had been unable to reach his potential on the track because of recurring physical problems but now would be given a chance to live up to his name, standing at stud at a farm in Tennessee. Bloodstock experts calculate that at best one out of five Thoroughbreds entering stud prove even moderately successful, but for a $5,000 ex-claimer stallion standing in a state that doesn't have legalized parimutuel horse racing, the odds must be millions to one. For Call Me Loverboy, those were short odds.

Selected Racing Records

Call Me Loverboy
bay, foaled 1997

By Gate Dancer out of Cupid's Way, by Lt. Stevens
Raced by J & J Stable, trained by Dan Arrigo

Racing from July of 1999 through April of 2004, Call Me Loverboy made 36 starts in a career compromised by injuries. He won 8 races, was second 6 times and third 3 times for earnings of $97,920. Loverboy ran in twenty-seven claiming races and was acquired by J & J Stable from a $62,500 claiming race on February 3, 2000. He finished his career by winning three of his final four races for J & J Stable, trained by Dan Arrigo.

Chindi
gray/roan, foaled 1995

By El Prado (Ire.) out of Rousing, by Alydar
Raced by CresRan Stable, trained by Steve Hobby

Chindi raced 81 times, with 18 wins, 13 seconds and 23 third-place finishes for earnings of $1,000,838. He ran in ten graded stakes and only once, his first time out, did he run in a claiming race. His most notable wins include the Grade 3 6-furlong Count Fleet Sprint Handicap at Oaklawn Park and the 7-furlong Grade 3 Ack Ack Handicap at Churchill Downs. He never ran beyond a mile; 54 of his races were at the common 6-furlong sprint distance, although according to his trainer his best distance may have been at the less frequently run distance of 6½ furlongs.

Dr. Robbie
chestnut, foaled 1997

By Doc's Leader out of Pretend to Stop, by Sham
Raced for numerous owners and trainers

Dr. Robbie ran 78 times from age 2 through 7, winning 18 races with 15 seconds and 7 third-place finishes for earnings of $196,869. Early in his career Dr. Robbie ran at 5½ and 6-furlong sprint distances but as he matured he ran in longer middle-distance and marathon races of up to a mile and ⅝. He ran in 52 claiming races and was claimed 10 times. He ended his career racing for Louis D. O'Brien and was trained by Ralph Martinez.

Fusto
bay, foaled 1999

By Majesty's Imp out of Nivin's Girl, by Ward McAllister
Raced for several owners and trainers

Fusto remained active through 2006, having won 9 of his lifetime 36 starts with 7 seconds and 3 third-place finishes for career-to-date earnings of $95,889. Early in his career he ran in non-claiming maiden special weight and allowance races, and competed in one stakes race, the 2002 Demetrisboy Stakes, limited to horses bred in Illinois. From 2003 on, Fusto ran almost exclusively in claiming races. From 2004 he raced for Louis O'Brien's Shamrock Stable, trained by Ralph Martinez.

Awholelotofmalarky
dark bay or brown, foaled 1998

By Dandy's Secret out of More Malarky, by Fifth Marine
Raced for Tower Farm, trained by Hector Magana and Jerry Calvin

Awholelotofmalarky raced 19 times from age 3 through 6, with 3 wins, 2 seconds and 3 third-place finishes for earnings of $98,410.

Glossary

Allowance Race A non-claiming race in which entered horses must meet certain restrictions, or "allowances." For example, an allowance race may be for horses who have not won a race other than a maiden race, or for horses who have not won two races other than a maiden race. Allowance conditions vary considerably and should be closely scrutinized by handicappers.

Broodmare A female horse used for breeding purposes.

Change Leads During the running of a race a Thoroughbred will grasp at the track with his left or right front foot. Changing leads, getting the horse to pull at the track with the opposite foot from which he is using, can sometimes give the horse an energy boost. Many jockeys will try to get their mount to change leads at the top of the stretch, especially if they sense their horse is tiring.

Claimer A horse that usually runs in claiming races.

Glossary

Claiming Race A race in which all the horses entered can be purchased, or "claimed," for a pre-determined price.

Classics Strictly defined, in the United States the Kentucky Derby, the Preakness and the Belmont Stakes. Loosely, any one of many high-profile, big-purse races, such as the Breeders' Cup Classic. Most countries have their own set of Classic races, e.g., the English Derby, the French Derby and others.

Colt A male horse under the age of five which has not been castrated.

Cross Maneuvering the reins to urge additional response from the horse.

Dam The broodmare, or mother, of a horse; e.g., Rousing is the dam of Chindi.

Eclipse Awards Awards made annually to outstanding equine and human participants in the Thoroughbred industry, similar to the *Oscars.*

Filly A female horse under the age of five.

Furlong An eighth of a mile. Most races in the United States are run at six furlongs, or ¾ of a mile. The Kentucky Derby is ten furlongs, the Preakness is nine and a half furlongs (a mile and three sixteenths), the Belmont Stakes is twelve furlongs, or a mile and a half.

Gate Jockey A rider who is habitually well-prepared for the beginning of a race and gets his horse away from the gate in good order.

Gelding A neutered, or castrated, male horse.

Handicap Race A race in which the racing secretary evaluates the equine entrants by their past performance and then assigns varying weights for each horse to carry. The assigned weights include the jockey. Horses with the best records carry the most weight. The concept is to give each horse in the race a chance to win regardless of ability by handicapping the better horses by requiring them to carrying more weight, a tiring influence.

Horse (Breeding definition.) A male horse five or older which has not been castrated.

Hot Box The sauna, used by jockeys to shed weight before races. One of a number of means employed by riders for weight reduction.

Length A term used to describe the distance between horses while racing. A length is the approximate length of a horse's body (roughly eight or nine feet). It is commonly recognized that it takes a Thoroughbred ⅕ of a second to run a length. A horse who loses a race by five lengths has therefore lost by a second.

Lugging In (Or lugging out.) Occurs when a horse begins to veer to his left (in) or to his right (out). Occurs most frequently when a horse begins to tire, is shying away from the use of the whip, or is in discomfort.

Maiden A racehorse of either sex which has never won a race.

Marathon Formerly a race of two miles or more, any race longer than a mile and a half is now generally considered a marathon.

Mare A female horse five years of age or older.

Middle Distance A race longer than a sprint, shorter than a marathon, informally between a mile and a sixteenth to a mile and a quarter, varying in different countries.

Odds-on When the betting payoff on a horse returns less than double the original bet, the odds are considered "odds-on." For example, if a $2 win bet returns a payoff of anything less than $4, it was an odds-on bet. Simply, it indicates a heavily favored horse.

Optional Claiming Race A race in which some but not all of the horses can be claimed if they meet certain performance or monetary eligibility restrictions.

Out A race. "The horse has had two outs this meet."

Pace The speed of the race. "The race had a hot (slow, average) pace."

Pickle A race horse of little monetary value.

Sire A male horse used for breeding; the equine father of a horse, e.g., Gate Dancer is the sire (father) of Call Me Loverboy.

Speed Rider A jockey who seems to prefer racing on the front.

Sprint A race of less than a mile, usually five, six or seven furlongs.

Stakes Race A race in which owners are required to put up an entry fee, or "stake." Generally, a stakes race features the highest quality competition. Stakes races vary by quality, the most prestigious being designated Grade I, II, or III, an evaluation which reflects the abilities of the entrants. Non-graded stakes races also feature exceptional horses but of a slightly lower classification. There are many exceptions to the rule.

Steam Box Sauna. See Hot Box.

Stretch The final portion of a race.

Tack Various equipment worn by horse and rider such as the saddle, girths, blinkers, protective vest, helmet, etc.

Triple Crown A series of three races run in the spring of each year for 3-year-old Thoroughbreds: The Kentucky Derby, the Preakness, and the Belmont Stakes.

Turf Race A race run on grass as opposed to dirt. In the United States most races are run on dirt. In Europe, nearly all races are run on grass.

Weanling A young Thoroughbred not yet a year old.

Wire The finish line.

Yearling A one-year-old Thoroughbred.

Index

Index

Index

Index